Nae Hair And A G String

By

Rod Macleod

Edited by Rod Macleod

Nae Hair and a G String - 1st Edition

Isbn : 978-0-9558509-0-5

Nae Hair & a G - String

Prologue

Mark Alexander Dexter, known to some as Mark, to others as Alexander, but to the Highlanders as 'Cyclops fanny features'. Mark started it all, it was his brainchild, and whatever is said about him in any derogatory nature will have to be ultimately overlooked. This is because he changed our lives forever & gave us the sort of memories that would always be up there with your 1st kiss, 1st shag, wedding day, divorce Party, looking at your newborn baby & receiving your foil wrapped special directors cut of Apocalypse Now dvd imported from the States.

Mark was not a big Man, he wasn't tall, maybe 5' 9" but quite heavily made, say about 190 lbs. He had dark hair, a fair complexion, eyes still sparkling & full of life set amidst a fat face. He liked to dress smart but casual, you know the type of person that would wear a shirt and tie constantly, but then counteract that with a pair of old jeans & a dark bomber jacket. He was always very business like & wanted to portray to people that he was a man with a purpose. Mark had always had business ideas & had tried his best to make them viable financial enterprises. His timing had always been bad though. He was usually in the wrong place at the wrong time. So he held down day jobs in the financial sector, working as a credit controller & various others clerical type jobs in accounts depts.He worked in the evening & at weekends as a personality disc jockey.He had that type of used car salesman personality, you know " How you doing today" ? not bad eh, " How would you like to be doing fantastically" ? "because I have got a deal of a lifetime, no I mean a LIFETIME, and I have it just for you, not for anybody else, just for YOU". So yes it was blah blah blah. Now it all comes down to there been two types of people in this world. The types that hate used car salesman with a vengeance. They think they are shallow, uncaring, loud, sleazy, dodgy individuals who would rob their grannies for a tenner. Or you could be on the other side of the coin where you think these guys are just like you ! salt of the earth. Out there like everybody else, trying to earn a buck, walking around with big smiles on there faces because well it's as survival instinct, isn't it ? they act that way because it is how they cope with life ! they have probably been shat on from a great height like most of us from time to time & sure they are trying to make money and they know they are loud & obnoxious, but hey they didn't ask to be born, but here we are, so enjoy the ride......(The band Keane sing the lyrics, "some people cry, some people lie, but it is just the way that we cope with our life's), (the anti - war movie platoon, which stars & is narrated by Charlie Sheen, comments on his brothers in arms, by saying The men that fought in Vietnam are not the rich boys, as they went to college & missed the draft.It was fought by poor men, men from the backwaters of Montana & from the poor areas of Mississippi & Idaho. These men were the best though & they could survive anything & there was not anything they could not take).

So why compare Mark James Reid to this ? Well Mark had tried & tried with his business ventures & just couldn't seem to get a break. What Mark didn't know though was that his time was coming ! He was about to start something that would get him & his next venture into every broadsheet & tabloid in Scotland, into magazines & onto radio & TV. Yes for once in his life Mark was in the right place at the right time, because the evolution of the Chippendales had started & they were coming to Scotland.........

One

"Out out, get yer f****ing cocks out", "Out out, get yer f****ing cocks out", the chant rose & rose from the packed function suite inside Stirling University. The Highlanders were three gigs into their "College & University" tour of Scotland. There was the full contingent that night, five strippers, a DJ plus his gopher, a road manager & of course Mark. The sound of Atlantic Oceans house anthem Waterfall was blasting out on the speakers & the crowd was starting to get restless. Dave the Highlanders faithfull DJ was pleading with the crowd to settle down " If you don't sit in yer f****in seats right now, the guys will not be coming on, so you won't see any f****in dicks & we'll all go home, so sit on yer arse". Dave was getting worried. He had recently been in a situation at a gig in Fife where the guys had taken that long to appear on stage that he had ended up getting the shirt ripped of him & his back had to be treated with ice cubes to cool down the plethora of scratches that had made a map on his back.

Mark was also worried, he was striding up and down inside the dressing room, wondering why he had ever thought up this whole malarkey & had agreed to get involved with this bunch of misfits. The misfits that he was referring to off course was the strippers. Five of the buggers, worse than bloody women, if they weren't putting gel in their hair, they were shaving their chest, or they were doing press-ups to give them a good pump before they went on stage or they were doing a nervous shit (Mark never understood this but the guys were always telling him that stage fright went straight to their ass & it was essential to unload before getting the g-strings on & he wouldn't want them farting in some poor unsuspecting women's face, bastards). They were already thirty minutes late & he was getting his ear bent by the organiser. Anyways He was sick of shouting at them, it just fell on deaf ears, sometimes they would just sit there, not even making a move to get ready, talking about why both Brutus & Levi had to insist on eating their pasta in the car on the way to the gig. Then fifteen minutes later, sure as fate they would start dropping their ass in the car & the windows would be down & the rest of the guys would be hanging out trying to get a bit of fresh. So enter stage left, that was where Marty came in. Marty was the Road Manager, which is a bit of a flamboyant title & the guys knew it. Marty was an ex-rocker who thought he still lived in the 70's, He had worked for a while in the Scottish Exhibition & Conference Centre in Glasgow, building stages for the bands travelling from all over the World. He would always boast that he had talked to Ozzi Osborne & Angus from Ac-Dc & personally knew & drunk with the full ensemble of Rush. The guys knew he was full of shit & had got fired from the SECC for stealing toilet paper from the loos. He was a friend of Mark's & Mark had needed somebody to get involved with all the organisation in sorting out the venues with lights etc, this was a pile of horseshit really, He had needed somebody to keep the guys in check. Although he was fastly learning that there was nobody that could keep the guys in check.

Marty was shouting at Brutus. Brutus was used to having Marty shouting at Him & was ignoring him as usual. Brutus was 6' 1" tall, all the Guys were at least 5' 11", with the tallest "Hero" being 6' 5". Brutus or Brutus T. Goldsmith (His full stage name), was a third American, a third Jewish & a third Scottish. His Mother was a Yank & had met his Dad in Poland when she had worked in the Fashion Industry. Well she was a seamstress & there had been a big contract for seamstress's in Krakow at the end of the Cold war. There had been a lot of movement of Russian workers in Poland & European & American workers were flocking in large numbers to get paid large sums for short periods of work. His mum had met His Dad who had been a Soldier and got married. When they were downsizing the Army, he had left & came to Scotland as a driver, which is what he had done in the army. Brutus's real name was Tom or Tommy & that is where the T came from. He got called Brutus by the other Guys in the Highlanders because Socrates said that he looked like Brutus out of the Popeye cartoon. He had a point, Brutus had one of these physiques, freaky natural genetics. He only worked out when he felt like it, which wasn't very frequently. He had a massive barrel chest, just like his Dad & forearms that seemed to be made of steel. His legs were like a couple of tree trunks & he had a chiseled muscular face with bright piercing blue eyes & a mop of jet black hair that he had spiked up like some sort of 80's punk & was a frightening sight. The women loved him though & he was a gentle giant.His real surname was Goldsmith, Mark had basically joint it all up & Brutus T Goldsmith the "gentle giant" was born.

"Move yer arse Brutus" Marty screamed, "Your always bloody last to get ready". "Shut it ya fud" Brutus replied, "I'll be ready when I'm ready". Levi or Levi Action slacks (full stage name), shouted over at Marty, "Marty I bet Ozzie never gave you this kind of hassle eh" ? "Shut it Action" replied Marty. Action was what Levi Action slacks used to get called back when Brutus was just called Brutus before He got ideas of Grandeur. Not content with just action & wanting a double barreled or triple barreled name. Well he always wore Levi's. He always commented how He had a 32" waist but had to buy 36" Levi's so that they would fit over his chunky legs. Well Levi's are slacks or so the American's say. So Levi action slacks was born. Levi was Glasgow born & had worked down the Sewers for nearly ten years before starting with the Highlanders. He had a real hang up about it & when out in the Town would tell all the chicks that He was an Accountant. They soon sussed out that he was talking pants though as he wasn't the sharpest tool in the box. What he lacked in brains though, He made up in physique. Unlike Brutus he worked his ass of in the gym. Usually four or five times a week. He had been training for twelve years & it showed. A very tight muscular upper body with a well defined back & triceps but legs that somehow looked like they belonged on another body. Levi agreed that his legs were not his best feature, but he always seemed to talk himself out of training them preferring to specialize on His upper torso. He had short cropped blonde hair, almost military style, with a thin face, bright green eyes with a strange yellow through them & a bright silver stud in his left ear. At 5' 11" he was the smallest in height of the strippers but had the natural boyish good looks to counteract it.

"You should be more like me fanny baws" Socrates shouted over to Brutus, "I was born ready". Brutus just grunted a reply & flipped Socrates the bird. Marty was getting really pissed off, his face was starting to glow a brighter shade of pink. He knew though that the guys would be ready for the choon before the choon. They always were, apart from that one time that Dog had run out of toilet roll & refused to go on stage until he could get another one. It was cool though, they just done a four man opener & dog had went on to do the first solo spot."You've got five" Marty shouted, but got no reply. So he sighed & went to find Mark. Mark was taking over from Dave. He always done a short spiel before the Guys went on.He was a DJ in the past though & sounded like Tony Blackburn on a good day, but like Tiger Tim that rest of the time. "Good evening ladies" Mark bellowed over the mic, He got no response so he tried again, "Good evening Ladies" he screamed. "F*** off & get the Guys on", one of the crowd retorted. Not phased Mark shouted "Are you all ready to see Scotland's Premier Male Dance troupe, the Highlanders" , once again no response. "Do you want to see Willie" he shouted over the mic, "Yessssssssssss" with various whoops & hollers responded the audience. "Well Willie's not here this evening" Mark joked "but i've got plenty of cock for you", this worked & the Women were screaming and shouting for more. "Who likes Uniforms" Mark screamed..........The Guys back in the changing room were listening to this & were nearly ready. They knew when to get their arse in gear. Dog asked Hero if it was the long intro or the short intro. Hero just grunted & shrugged his shoulders. Hero was known for his shoulders, they were like a couple of cannonballs on top of his torso. He was the tallest of the group at 6' 5" tall, he was an impressive sight. He had the perfect body, everything was in proportion. Even his massive shoulders would have looked silly if they had been smaller. He had been a Scottish Bodybuilding champion that had gone on to doing quite well in the amateur competitions down South but had missed out in getting his Pro Card a few times & now just settled to maintaining his massive physique & doing His stripping, which was no mean thing considering that the Guys were out on the job four or five nights a week travelling all over the Country. He had also managed to give up his door job, which made him happy as there was always some asshole that wanted to square up to him because of his size. He also had a blonde ponytail which completed his whole stripper image. The only thing that Mark complained about was that he refused to take sun beds and would not use tanning creams. So yes he might have been the whitest stripper in Scotland but with his sheer size, got away with it.

The lush sounds of the song before the song wallowed there way around the dressing room The guys were putting on their Highlanders jackets. Black bomber style jackets with gold embroidery spelling out "The Highlanders". They were all wearing kilts representing the various clans, although none of them actually knew what clans they were sporting. Not because they weren't patriotic, just because they weren't that interested. Tourists to Scotland always seem to be under the impression that Scots know everything about their Ancestors & many actually believe that we still jump around in the kilts & that we all have red hair. Dog had red hair, well He wouldn't actually admit it was red, more kind off strawberry blonde. But to the Guys he was a ginge & always would be. Dog was the most unlikely stripper amongst them. When the guys had first met him, not only had he a ginger barnet but he had a middle parting ginger barnet. Dog had the real rough & ready looks. He had been a bit of a lad in his day & and had quite a bad mars bar on his coupon where he had got mixed up with Arthur Thompson jnr lot. He had seemingly been on the opposing side & had stepped into the wrong bar one night on his tod. So that is how he got his scar & also earned his name. So he brought that in with him & it just stuck. He had seen a decent surgeon about a year before joining up with the Highlanders & got the scar sorted. It was still slighty visible though but added to his whole ruggish good looks & demeanor. Dog didn't really work out with weights, He had been a decent amateur boxer in his day & still done some sparring. He had got the middle parting sorted into a crew cut, had a good tight but slight build, a few tattoos & at 6' 2" looked impressive.

Dog, Hero & Socrates rolled up the sleeves of their Highlander jackets & Brutus & Levi kept theirs down. They all had tight black t-shirts on under the jackets. Dave the DJ was back on the mic "Ladies, for one night only, it's Scotland's Premier Male dance troupe, the Highlanders". Socrates was the first man on stage, followed in unison by the other four strippers. They lined up with their back to the crowd. The women were going radio rental. The lights on stage went out & simultaneously the spot lights fell on the five statues, sending eerie shadows dancing on the far wall like mannequins doing a jig in a shop window late at night. "Are you ready for this" sung the lead singer of 2 Unlimited, as the strippers swung into action.

Two

Socrates opened his eyes. It was Saturday the 1st of February 1997. He was in a B & B in a small village on the west coast of Scotland called Ballahoulish, not far from Fort William. It was a two horse town in the middle of nowhere & Socrates loved doing these gigs. When he had arrived the night before, the whole village had been in darkness. All you could make out was the silhouettes of the houses against the night sky. What he had not realised though was that the village had a mountain backdrop & when he peered through his bedroom curtains they stared down at him, frowning with their white hats, as the winter snow was still gathered & the mist hung lazily over their peaks. The Highlanders had some strange bookings in their time, a string of bingo hall gigs, showcases in shopping centres on a Saturday afternoon, with boyfriends & husbands getting dragged about wearily with girlfriends & wife's, they gapped with their mouths hanging open as five strange looking big dudes jumped about in kilts & black t - shirts, that looked five times too small for them, grabbing a few unsuspecting grannies & the girls with the shortest skirts on, more like a face cloth wrapped around their bum and doing obscene things to them in the middle of the shopping mall floor - Poofs ! They had performed in Indian Restaurants, proving to the women that "you can't curry love" & "poppadom don't preach", some of the women were having naan of it as well ! They had made appearances for high street shops, with JFS (Jeans for Sale) being a one time sponsor. They had done snooker clubs, giving a new meaning to the term "potting a long pink". This time though took the biscuit. They had been booked to appear on the 31st January 1997 in a museum, yes that's correct, a museum. Ballahoulish had a national heritage centre/ museum & we had been booked to appear there. Turned out we weren't getting our boabies oot amongst the Corinthian & ionic columns of the impressive building, no they had a function suite at the back. Just as well the idea of getting your tackle out with William Wallace & Robert the Bruce watching us, sends shivers down our spine.

Socrates closed his eyes again, left it for another couple of minutes & then opened them again. No it did not make any difference, he still felt like shit ! He had drunk a lot of alcohol after the gig, they all had. They usually took advantage of these type of gigs, you know, weekend gigs where a hotel or B & B was involved to have a wee swally. This had not been a wee swally though, they had all been drinking for the UK. Turned out the guy who had organised the gig, was also a local MP. a bouncer on a hotel door (these small villages didn't have nightclubs you see, it was always hotels which had a late Licence & double up as a disco) & he owned a b & b. Seemingly in these small rural places this was very common for someone to have three or four jobs. It was how they made ends meet. Kept the wolves from the door. Quite literally speaking in a place like this. They had been invited into the sitting room of Archibald's B & B. His lovely wife Gemima had brought the guys sandwiches & tea & coffee. Then had made her goodnight & left the men to talk. The guys found this quite strange, but realised that must be "their way" up here & did not say anything to embarrass Archie

(Archibald). He had been a wonderful host & they had sat up to the wee small hours downing whisky, gin & vodka. Archie was a hardened drinker & the guys found it hard keeping up with him. It was great to cut loose though, the guys had a really busy December with the silly season & all & did not get much time to chill out. They were making up for it now though. They all knew though that they were working the next night in Glasgow & that they would regret it in the morning. It was worth it though as Archie's eyes were gleaming, His big red face was beaming also, it had been a good night for him. The gig had been a sell out, he had made a small fortune on the door with the proceeds going to fix the clock on the church tower & the bar tills had been ringing all night. He knew that he had taken a gamble booking these lads, the religious element in Ballahoulish was strong, the Wee Free's had control of the village since the last great war & they were not tumbling to the pressures of modern day society & their evil materialistic ways. So he had been sweating for a long time that the boys were going to be met by the village priest & an angry placard carrying mob behind Him. His master stoke of course had been to offer the profits though to priest Mcflannery & his ailing clock on the tower of the church. That was what saved his bacon & he knew it. So this night sitting with the strippers was as much a case for celebrating for him as it was for them to grab a rest. The strange thing was though, that the guys were to experience this same event in about five Years in Stornoway, where once again they would face the old world & be reminded of Ballahoulish.

Socrates rolled his legs out of bed, stood up & then immediately sat down again. The room was spinning. Why oh why did he drink so much last night. Tonight's gig was going to be a nightmare. He stood back up, went for a piss, farted & stared into the mirror. A long face with deep brown eyes, chestnut brown hair, short & untidy stared back. He walked back into the room & tried to find his boxers, couldn't find them, so just shrugged & pulled on his Jeans. He smelled his arm pits, they seemed ok but couldn't be sure, so he gave them a quick blast of Brut aquatonic & and threw on the same white t - shirt as last night. He always wore white t- shirts or white shirts & faded jeans. The guys gave him a hard time about it but he didn't care. he liked white & he liked jeans, so f*** it. Anyways Brutus always wore black t -shirts & bloody combat trousers all the time. He laughed to Himself, Brutus would always go quiet when they started to rib him about his dress sense, Brutus knew that he would be next on their agenda hahaha ! Socrates had the total opposite body of Levi, He had massive legs, like the American bodybuilder Tom Platz. They were huge, He had to go to outsize shops to get jeans to fit him, Tall & Mighty and shops like that. His upper body was still good but got overshadowed by His legs. The guys just called him Legs & He quite like it. He used to have skinny pins as a Boy & he got these big babies by sheer hard work. He used to squat till he puked & he definitely thought of himself as Hardcore. Outside the gym though he was quite a shy guy & was very self conscious of his size & would cover up his upper body with white shirts & a jacket. He had worked in a golf ball factory, putting the dimples on golf balls & checking that the correct number of dimples were on the balls. He had been called a Dimpler & anybody that he met would get told that he was a Dimpler but couldn't tell them what that meant as it was a secret. People used to just think that he worked in a golf ball factory, putting dimples on golf balls. His real name was Brent, when he was at School, He used to get called Bent or Bent boy, which was one of the reasons he started to use weights at the age of fourteen. He had thought up the stagename Socrates, nobody knew why. Mark had liked it & had thought it was something to do with his fascination of Greek Mythological figures but had never said. So he just got called Legs or Socks or sometimes Bent boy.

He gave Dog a kick, who he was sharing the room with, Dog grunted "what" & Socks replied "breakfast". He went downstairs to find out he was first up. That was no surprise, he was usually always first up & Hero was usually always last up. Gemima was busying herself setting the breakfast table & said good morning to socks & enquired if he had slept ok. "Yes thanks", "It's nice to wake up somewhere quiet, instead of sunny old Glasgow, although my head is not very quiet at the moment". Gemima just smiled a reply. She did not seem phased to have five male strippers sleeping under her roof plus a DJ. Mark and Marty & Gloves had not been with the Guys the previous night. Gloves was the gother.He got called Gloves because he wore driving gloves all the time. It's not as if he drove a Porsche, He drove a beat - up Peugeot 305 estate. The Guys made his life a living hell & he was happy to get a night off. Gemima was a small women, very clean & proper looking. Whereas her husband was a big man, big & burly & in charge. Socks smiled to himself as he looked around the dining room, he imagined Gemima wearing nothing but her pinny & spanking Archie on the bum with her big feather duster as he wore nothing except one of the G -strings he had "borrowed" from the Highlanders the night before. Gemima continued busying about bringing out cereal & butter & jam & asking Socks if he wanted the full monty ? "Excuse me" Socks said surprised. "The Full Monty" repeated Gemima smiling, "do you want a full grill up", "I know you Guys are too healthy to have a fry up". "I don't know about that laughed Socks, not after the drinking we done last night". Gemima was acting as if she had male strippers under her roof every weekend, thought Socks. He liked feeling special & realised that one of the most important parts of his job was just speaking to people & giving them a laugh, taking them away from their everyday life's just for a short time. Then sometimes he felt he was being vain & pompous feeling like that. It was hard not to have an ego in this game, especially when you have been a Dimpler in your previous life. People used to always say to the Guys that they were always surprised and delighted that they were all laid back dudes & didn't have airs & graces. Why should we have Hero used to say, we just take our clothes of for a living, it's not as if we are doctors or anything, saving peoples lives.

Socks walked around the back of the dining room table & stared out through the long rectangular window. The mountains loomed up in front of Him. He just stood their for a minute staring at them. They had a majestic beauty. They had stood their for hundreds of years & would stand for hundreds to come. Life in the village would bustle about, or as much bustling that you can get in Ballahoulish, but these mountains would just stand & stare. He wondered if the villagers even noticed the mountains any more & whether they would just stop & be like him staring at them or whether they just took them for granted. Suddenly something caught socks eyes & he looked down & looked puzzled for a minute & then laughed out loud. He decided though not to say anything to the other guys. Let the fun commence.

Next down was Brutus, "awright ya fud" Brutus said to Socks, "no" replied Socks, "my head is banging, hows yours", "it's been better" replied Brutus. The guys all appeared one by one over the next ten minutes & exchanged the usual greetings "awright baw jaws", "morning ya fanny", "awright fanny baws". The only person that wasn't there was Hero as usual. "Dog, go give him a shake" said Brutus. "F*** him" said Brutus, "let him go hungry" "I'll get him" said Socks. Another ten minutes passed & Hero appeared looking the worse of wear. "About time ya fud" said Dave. Hero didn't reply, just took his place at the table. Gemima came out & asked Hero if he wanted the full monty. All the guys fell about laughing & Hero just look confused, obviously oblivious to the new in joke. All the other guys had been fed & were just finishing of the last slices of toast & downing the strong black coffee. Socks loved coffee & he liked it strong, this was good strong coffee & he was on his third cup. Dave & Socks had been giggling away like wee school boys ever since Dave had appeared. The Guys were just ignoring them as they couldn't be arsed asking what they were up too. They were all feeling rough. Archie wasn't there as he had agreed to go round to the Museum early to help clear up from the night before. Gemima was in the kitchen doing the washing up already. "Whit aboot the Basookas on that wee red head" said Brutus. "Never mind her" said Dave did you clock the pins on that big blonde", "I love these short skirts". The Guys all fell about laughing. That was one of the Highlanders wee quirps, one of their "essential sayings". Dave and a couple of the Guys had been down in Blackpool for a long weekend a few years back. They had been in some cafe on the promenade & the waitress serving them had a short skirt on. Dave had just come out with it right in front of Her. "I love these short skirts" he had said & the other two guys had just looked at each other amazed & then at Him & then at her in unison & she had just smiled & walked back to the cash desk as the three of them rolled about laughing. "No way" one of the Guys had said, "I can't believe you just said that". "Yeah last night was world class" said Hero, that was another essential saying & had to be said with a certain lilt to the word "class" "world classssssssssss". The Guys all laughed again apart from Hero, He was staring out of the window with his mouth wide open. "What the f****" he gasped. Then he looked at Dave & Dave couldn't hold it in any longer, He was howling, greeting & the tears were running down his eyes & he was convulsing in fits of laughter. He was at the opposite side of the table than Hero, Hero jumped up & ran round the table to get him, but the wee man was short and wiry & faster than the big lump, he was under the table in a flash & up over the other side. He horsed it to the front door & was out into the small car park & round the side of the building in a flash. Hero was after him & the two of them disappeared from view from the front window. The guys could still hear Dave laughing though &

Hero huffing & puffing after him.

Socks was also falling about laughing at the side of the table. He was looking at the other three guys & they were just staring back at him with "what the f**** is going on in their eyes". Socks was holding his sides & said "Look, look at , at the car, the car park" he gasped ! The other Guys looked at the car park & one by one the realisation came over their faces. Out in car park was Hero's car & Gloves car. Ok you know glove wasn't there, but Brutus's car was in the garage getting fixed & had borrowed Glove's car. He had his back to the window & had not seen it. The Guys had taken two cars, one for all the PA gear & the gig gear with Brutus & Dave in one car & the other four guys in Hero's Car. The thing was when they got to the gig which was half a mile away at the other side of the village. They had left both cars there & had started drinking at the gig & were unable to drive afterwards. All except Dave who had just one pint at the gig & was saving himself to later. Dave had just passed his driving test the previous week & had been pleading with Hero to give him a shot of his car. Hero's love & joy was his car. He had a Ford Capri Brooklands 3.0L special edition. Plenty of people had the 2.8L version. Not him, They only made five hundred models of the Brooklands & it was a collector's edition. It had a reconditioned engine, twin exhaust pipes & 17" alloy wheels. It had full black leather with a leather steering wheel & gear stick knob. It had an expensive sound system & Hero washed it by hand at least twice a week. Hero had told Dave that he had two chances of getting a shot "No hope & Bob Hope". So Dave had just waited for his chance when the guys had finished the show & had driven them piled in to Gloves Peugeot, dropped them off at the B & B & told them He was going to sort his CDs & vinyl back into there cases. The guys just thought he was in his room, phoning his new wee bird, Mary-Bell. Dave wasn't really like the rest of the Guys. He was pretty shy when it came to females. Sure he would window shop but he wouldn't buy.So the guys just fought he was pulling his chugger while speaking to Mary-Bell on the phone. What he had really done of course was to dip Hero's jacket pocket & walk the half mile back to gig & then drive back in Hero's baby.

The guys were all falling about laughing watching Hero chasing Dave around the car park. Dave was soon back inside, locking himself in the toilet, while Hero was walking around his car inspecting it for scratches & dents. Dave was a bad driver you see. Very reckless, very irresponsible. Anyways one & half hours later the Guys had been washed & dressed, had said their goodbyes to Archie & Gemima & the mountains & were back on the road. It was midday & the guys knew that they had to be in Glasgow for eight- thirty that night. They had eight & a half hours to recover & they all had mouths like an Arabs sannie & were feeling salty. Dog & Socks in the back seat of the Capri were asking Hero to slow down as he horsed around the curves & bends heading towards Tarbert & Loch Lomond. They were feeling queasy, they were not good passengers. Dave was just glad he was in Gloves car with Brutus.They both laughed about the morning's events as they turned right at the Tarbet hotel onto the Loch Lomond road . The car followed the white lines on the road hypnotising it's passengers until the familiar houses & offices & shops of suburbia loomed up before them in the distance & brought them back to reality. It was 2.15pm. They had six hours & fifteen minutes to rest, eat, get their gear ready for tonight's performance. One thing for is for sure, Socks knew that the following morning He would be awaking to the high rises of Sighthill, not the glorious mountains of Ballahoulish. Then again he might get lucky tonight.

Three

There are many pizza franchises in the World, Pizza Express, Pizzaland & Pizza Hut to name a few, but it is the unofficial franchise of Pizza Hut in Barrhead that will always retain fond memories for the Guys. It wasn't actually a Pizza making establishment at all, in fact it was a Community Centre. It was also where all the Guys originally met & where they honed their dance moves every Saturday & Sunday for four Months. I don't remember why we called it the Pizza Hut, We just did. It was the sort of thing we done. Somebody would say it once & it would just stick. So yeah this was more or less where it all started. The bunch of misfits got organised & became an organised bunch of misfits. Well as organised as misfits can get with Dog & Hero onboard.

So it was one lazy, wet Saturday afternoon in Glasgow. Rangers & Celtic were playing an early kick-off and the traveling through to Barrhead was slow & frustrating. We all got there eventually though, even Hero had made a special effort & got there only thirty minutes late. All the usual introductions were made, Mark was in His element. He was addressing everybody together & telling them the rundown for the afternoon. He & Marty were going to take each Guy one at a time into a separate room & ask Him to remove His top to check that they had a good enough body to get past the first hurdle. He would then be very apologetic& say that He would have to see the Bishop to make sure that it passed the size test. I think that we were all very nervous about this & were making various small talk (Who do you think will win today's game, what Gym do you train in, where do you live, do you socialise in the town, etc). Everybody passed the initial checks & relaxed a bit until phase two. Phase two was where a Choreographer from Stirling was coming through to see if we had the necessary dance moves. Mark had informed us that we did not have to be great dancers but just had to have at least a sense of rhythm. I think we were all pretty worried about that also, we were all pretty big Guys & some Guy was going to arrive shortly & go all Wayne Sleep on us. His name was Junk Stowrage & He had been delayed by the football traffic but would be there in fifteen minutes. So we all just sat around & made small talk & sized each other up. God we were an unusual bunch. To a normal Joe in the Street we would have looked really strange.I suppose I didn't really think that we looked that strange. Then again I knew that I was eccentric in my own way. Certainly my whole Family were quite strange & eccentric, so it was sometimes hard to spot these same traits in other People.

There was a Guy wearing these Baggy Jogging pants that a lot of Bodybuilders wear. It said Gold's Gym down the side & He wore a fanny bag (as the Yanks call it), slung around at the bottom of His waist. You know, for keeping your money, keys, photo of your sweetheart etc.He reminded me of that Guy who sung "Word Up" although He wasn't wearing a red pair of pants over his Baggies & He wasn't black. Another Guy was wearing a pair of Rupert the Bear check trousers & and a Black waistcoat & Jamiriqui style hat. Then there was the dude with the green & brown Barber jacket & a pair of brown leather boots with buckled straps on the side & the flaps turned down like Bono out of U2 used to wear. As I sat there and took these Guys in, all I could keep thinking was that we looked like some oversized version of the audition of the characters out of Fame. The Guy with the Rupert trousers on had been last to go into the room for the body & boabey test. He came back into join the rest of us looking quite pleased with Himself. As we all had done. It is not every day you are asked to slap your tackle out to a couple of Guys & get told "yes thank you Old Chap, that will do the job nicely". I don't know about the rest of the Guys but I had definitely worn a pair of extra - tight boxer trunks that day & was given the wee chap a wee shimmy shammy in my pocket with my left hand before I went in for my turn & received the "Yes that will suffice Old Boy". For all the females I have ever slept with in my day, I don't recall every hearing these immortal words again "Yes that will suffice Old Boy". Then there was the Guy in the light coloured crimpoline trousers & the Fred Perry top that went out of fashion ten years earlier. He had on a pair of shoes that looked like they belonged on a different person, they were absolutely massive. I remember when I met Him, all I could do was stare at His feet. I thought He was some kind of freak, turned out I was right He was our DJ. Dick or Dave or something. What He didn't know then was that He was going to spend ten years of His life watching us getting our dicks out.

Junk Stowrage had arrived at the Hut. Mark was having a hurried word in His shell like. It Turned out that they were both Mates. I think they had been involved in some Business Venture in the past. He introduced Junk to us & we got down to Business. The first choon that He wanted us to burst a few moves to was Right said Fred "I'm too sexy". We really wore that choon out, infact we played it that much that one of the Guys got hypnotised by it & used it in one of His routines for Years. So there was the five of us in a row, getting ready to get down to it. At this point I would just like to point out that if you are having a "Full Monty" moment with the Guys in the factory and Robert Carlyle's Son working the tape deck. Can I just say that we made these Guys look good. We were a Simon Cowell wet dream, He would have obliterated us. If Simon Cowell had been the Choreographer that day, the Highlanders would not have been born. We would have probably all got normal jobs & have gone on to lead normal lives. It wasn't Simon Cowell though, It was Junk Stowrage. He just kind of sighed & turned to Mark & said that there was a lot of hard work ahead. One by one He took us through the moves. I don't really know what He said to everybody individually. Certainly It was easy to spot that some of us had a more natural rhythm & others couldn't dance for love or money. What Junk said to me was "You can't dance but you can grind". Certainly the much underrated skill of grinding should not be underestimated as this is the backbone of a Strippers bread & butter. Junk would always say to me, "Master the fingers & thumbs & your toes will follow".

"Wild Boys, Wild Boys" W-W-W-Wild boys" Dog look perplexed as He tried to maintain the upper arm coordination in unison with raising and lowering His legs. No, No No screamed Junk at Dog. "Dog your not Taking your great Dane a walk in the bloody park you know", "You too Socrates, you would give an epileptic a bad name, you have as much rhythm & coordination in your Body as Woody Allen on acid". The Guys all fell about laughing. Junk wasn't laughing though. This was the third weekend in the row, the fifth bloody session He had spent with these reprobates & He was getting tired. Nearly as tired as Simon Le Bon's "Wild Boys" vocals. "Chill Homey" Dog retorted to Junk, "at the end of the day, they will all go wild, wild, wild in the Country when they see our boabeys". The Guys all laughed again. It was good bringing some levity into the Hut. They had been spending four hours each weekend. Two on a Saturday & two on a Sunday. They knew it would get worse before it got better. They were getting to know each other pretty well & they were all starting to click with one another. Mark had been busy planning full shows (Full Shows are two hour fully contained events, where the venue would get four or five strippers plus a DJ & MC including full PA for a fixed price. Other times the Venue would work on a door price deal, where the act would get a percentage of the door takings). The first full show would be in a couple of Months & we had to be ready. He had been talking to various Newspapers & a PR Company called "Take the Bait".There was other strippers out there working the scene & we had all been either individually or in two's sent along to do either one or two individual spots (an individual spot is where just one male stripper goes onstage at a time for a duration of fifteen minutes). So we had all plodded along to these first night experiences & yes we had filled our drawers. We had stood there shaking, shivering wrecks. Then we had been announced onstage by the DJ & we had walked onstage, totally forget about all the moves we were shown & just make a total utter dick of ourselves as we ran around and ruffled a few hairdo's & used about fifteen women in the routine when it was meant to be two. We have removed all our clothes in about sixty seconds & then wondered what the hell we would do for the next fourteen minutes. Yet the Women didn't seem to care. They still went mental.

I had never seen Women act like this. They were wild beasts, unleashed from Society in general & escaping from the day to day truggery of modern day life. They were all Women together with no Men to judge them or make catty or hurtful comments to them. They were a tribe, a cult of boabey hungry She Devils. They were going to feed tonight & the male strippers were going to be their prey. They would lavish in baby oil & whipped cream. They would be handcuffed & have sex simulated on them on the dance floors. Then they would want their Mates to have the same treatment. They would drink as if they would never drink again (PLEASE REMEMBER TO DRINK RESPONSIBILY AT HIGHLANDER SHOWS AS WE DO NOT ADVOCATE THE RISE OF THE LADETTE). They would then go Home to their Husbands and Boyfriends, unsuspecting of what was shortly to come. They would be quietly watching "Where Eagles Dare" or some late night Comedy show. "Hey how come you've got Brutus written on your tits with a magic marker" ? "Hoi whits this on your Ass "Her" who the hell is "Her" ? "It's Hero dafty" would reply the wife, "He left the "O" out over my bum hole. Then the Wife/ Girlfriend would shag the arse right of Her Man & She would be content & He would send Her out to many more strippers nights, because He now knows that there is a way of getting a good rogering without it having to be His Birthday. The thing was if they act like this when we are total shite, how will they act when we are just really bad ?

The Door of the first hall of the Pizza Hut burst open & three teenage girls peeked in "Are yous these strippers bye the way" ? giggle giggle, "Aye we are these strippers doll" replied Levi. "Get yer kit of then big Boy" retorted the teenager. "I think you're a bit young for that doll face" replied Levi. Mark appeared just then "Whit are you three wanting, go on piss off". We got this a lot. There was usually netball or football or something or the other going on in the other hall. So there was these constant interruptions. Not that we bothered it just got to be part of the Pizza Hut experience. Junk Stowrage was getting to busy to come through from Stirling every weekend because of other Commitments. Actually we think that He had just had enough of us & was at breaking point. You couldn't blame the man, we could give a headache a sore head. So we got a replacement. Her name was Sonia Blitz, She was a brunette about 5'5", quite attractive with a nice figure. She the first of four female Choreographers. She was a good Kid, about twenty two. She had thick skin, which was a must working with us clowns & we developed thick skin in return, as She was going to work the ass's right of us. It was the best thing that could have happened getting a chick in like that. Suddenly we were all turned up on time, apart from Hero that is. Well He was only fifteen minutes late rather than thirty, so it was an improvement. She would give us pelters & we would take it, no back chat like there had been with Junk. We just paid attention & built up a good rapoire with Sonia. We actually got Her in the Newspapers once with us. We were doing a photo shoot up in some Moors in the middle of nowhere. Take the Bait had set it up & we were to just be bare upper bodied with the kilts on & Sonia was wearing an evening dress with a big feather boyar. It was bloody freezing as it was the middle of Winter. Take the Bait had wanted lots of different angle shots for their Portfolio, so we were there for what seemed like an age. "I've got goose pimples on my goose pimples" said Socks. Dave just stood around smiling at us with his big shoes. He had looked pretty bored for the first month or so in the Pizza Hut. Can't blame Him really all He was really doing was sitting at the Tape Deck, pressing play, stop, pause, rewind, play, pause, rewind, pause, play, fast forward, stop. He had a right good laugh at our expense though, watching us ballsing it up time after time.

Sonia was in no mood today for farting about. She had two more weeks to get the opening routine ready. The first full show was just around the corner. The Highlanders had been booked for a Bingo Hall in Stirling & Socks still couldn't get the f***ing opening moves right. "di di di di di di di , di di di di di di di, are you ready for this" screamed the lead singer of 2unlimited. "Socrates you are still a full beat too early, remember what I told you, count it out in your head 1,2,3,4,1,2,3,4. "Sorry Sonia" replied Socks. "I don't know what your laughing at Brutus" said Sonia, "at least He's not visually counting the beats with His mouth","what have I told you, you cannot get away with doing that in a live situation". Brutus said nothing, just looked at the floor in a bashful kind of way.

The truth was that we were all guilty of doing the number counting thing & infact we were probably doing it in our sleep. The harsh reality was though that we had to sort it & quick. We were going live, three group routines. One at the start of the show, one in the middle & one at the end & we had two weeks to get it right.

Four

The lights changed from amber to green, Hero hit the gas, his white Opel Manta with go-faster red stripes groaned & jerked into submission & sped off. It was a 1.6L model with black alloys. It was actually very similar in design & handling to the much larger engine 3.0L Capri that He would own years later. It had the same big nose & the same slanty rear view windscreen that made it difficult to park, until you got used to driving the baby. What a baby she was, she was a cherry. Hero had got the 1.6L engine chipped & had given it another twenty horses. Then he had put on a chrome exhaust, we all loved this exhaust. Think about one of the cannon's at Edinburgh castle & you will get an idea of the size of the bugger. Anways seemingly this cannon added another ten horses onto the power of the brief. So all in all She was a hundred and twenty bhp vehicle. It was really a 2+2 coupe, you know enough room in the back for two small children, not two big bloody bears ie Brutus & Levi. With Socks in the front with Hero driving of course. Nobody got to drive his cherry, his peach.

It was the fourteenth of March 1991, Friday, 6.30pm. We had all met in the car park of the Water Mill Hotel in Paisley. Mark & Disco Dave & Gloves all came from Paisley. The rest of us all resided in reasonably nearby surrounding areas & it seemed an agreeable place as any to rendezvous. All in all there were three cars that night. Disco Dave & Gloves were together with the entire PA & were sitting behind the manta. Mark & Marty & Dog were setting the pace up front & were just pulling onto the M8 at the David Lloyd junction. The tail end of the Friday peak time traffic was tailing off. Most people try and finish that bit earlier if possible on a Friday. They will work on just that little bit extra Monday to Thursday to get away that extra hour or two on a Friday. Party time plans or spending extra time with the kids or heading off for the weekend. Whatever their reasons it was benefiting the guys. It was there first full show & they were heading to Stirling. The Mecca bingo hall was to be where it all started & was also to be the start of a long & happy relationship with Mecca, with the Guys working all over Scotland in many of their chains. The nights were starting to get lighter a little later with Spring creeping in. There was just a little cloud cover that night, but the sky was mainly clear. The mood in the three cars was fairly similar, there was an underlying atmosphere of tension. Yes the strippers were nervous, they were nervous about making an ass of themselves. The DJ was nervous, He was nervous that the cds would stick, that his amp would fuse & that his speakers would explode. Glove's was nervous, he was nervous that he would grab the wrong things of the stage that should not be grabbed & that he would leave the things on stage that should have been grabbed. Marty was nervous that the Strippers, Dave & Glove all made an arse of it & made him look bad in turn.

The person that was the most nervous of course was Mark. He was bricking it. He had a put a lot of resources into this & as yet had got nothing back. He kept telling himself, you have to speculate to accumulate. He hated that saying, it always meant that you were going to be skint for bloody ages before you saw a jelly bean. He had paid for the hire of the Pizza Hut, He had paid for the time of both choreographers (although he got a good discount for Junk), he had paid for outfits, these bloody jackets had cost a fortune because of the gold embroidery and he still had to pay Levi's contact in the fashion game the other half of the money & the guy was getting heavy with him on the phone. Levi had been giving him grief about it, "Mark, Harvey has been on the bloody phone again man, when are you going to pay him the balance for the jackets" ? , "Levi, I told him he'll get the dosh after the first couple of gigs", then he had to pay Take the Bait three hundred for that bleeding photo shoot in the marshes plus another couple of deals. They wanted more money as well & now. He couldn't mess them around, they were an above-board high street professional PR Company, they could make his life a living Hell. Never mind though, it wasn't all bad, he was getting a grand for the gig tonight. The new stripper dudes were only getting £40 each although he was going to have to pay a couple of the old timers the full dough of £80, he didn't just want to rely on the Highlanders, not just yet, they might be really bad, he didn't know what to expect, so he had hired a wee piece of insurance via the two old timers who he knew would rock the shop & if it all went pear shaped, save the day. He had got Dave & Glove's for a song, £40 for the two of them, he had promised to up Dave's money after a couple of shows, but would see how long he could hang it out for. As far as he knew Dave was just giving Glove a tenner. What did he care. He was getting away with giving Marty £20, that was fine with Marty as long as Mark slipped him a length later. So that was £420 in total overheads for the night, throw in another £20 in petrol, that's a tenner each for Hero & Gloves cars, so £440 all in. So that was £560 in Mark's back tail, ching ching ! Of course the guys didn't know that Mark was getting paid a fat grand. He had told them it was £600.

"Fat lying bastard" said Levi in the back of the Manta, "He's still fannying Harvey on about the jackets, The guys been on the blower to me about fifty times already", "what about Heather at McTavish & McShuggle" complained Socks, "She got these kilts ready for us in four days", "He still owes her half the bloody money", the guys all laughed apart from Brutus. "He still owes me a tenner petrol for that bloody photo shoot in Timbuktu" moaned Hero. "Ten pound already" said Levi, "five pound alreadies", "what do you want two pound for", the guys all laughed again apart from Brutus. The guys had very quickly worked out that Mark was a bullshit artist of the highest quality. They think that he had watched the movie "Wall Street" one day & it had been a defining moment in his life. Unfortunately It was just a little bit too high a standard to set for yourself when your a tight lying bastard. This was another of the phrases that would be repeated with glee for many years by the guys. Mark used to always say, "what do ya want a tenner for", "I'll give you a fiver". "Yeah he nearly choked that day at the Pizza Hut where we couldn't get in for two hours & had to fire round to Disco Dave's old dears house & when we eventually got in, we were all starving, so we sent him out for sandwiches & when he realised that he wasn't getting any readies he went all bleary eyed" laughed Socks, all the guys were roaring with laughter apart from Brutus. "Hey Brutus" shouted Hero from the front over the top of Pete Tong's essential new choon, "what's up with yer puss", "you've not cracked a light all night, were all nervous you know dude", "but that's not the reason I'm quiet", "what's up with you Bro" said Levi, "I was out last night at the Subbie" retorted Brutus, "and well, I didn't mean to you know Mon, but I kind of got full of sweeties, a lot like, and then when I got in I hammered some jellies and I still feel kind of wired to the moon man". Silence fell on the Opel for about twenty seconds, all you could here was some bird singing about how she lost her man, but that she knew she was a bitch, and that life was a bitch, and she didn't have any money, and that he wasn't getting another chance.LIFES A BITCH she would keep telling the listener. The words just kept digging into the passengers brains, it even drowned out Hero exhaust, which had a habit of waking his neighbours at four in the morning when he returned from a hard nights clubbing.

The silence ended.........."You stupid f***ing wanker" shouted Hero from the front over Pete trying to tell his listeners about where various A list wanker DJs who got paid exuberant amounts of money to play other peoples records were going that evening to ply there wears." Our first gig, Our first f****ing gig & you go out & get wired, you total asshole, wanker, fanny", "I'll be ok" replied a very humble Brutus, "I'll be fine", "you c**t" said Levi, "you fanny f*** asshole dog breath bollocks baws" shouted Socks from the front of the car over Pete still trying to make himself heard. "Listen guys I'll be ok, I'll be fine, I will, I'll be ok" shouted Brutus. He was feeling really strange though, oh he wished he hadn't gone out, but he was feeling so nervous, just sitting in and thinking about it & Budgie kept phoning him & pleading with him to go. He closed his eyes, all he could hear was the assault of verbal abuse from the guys. "wanker, fanny, asshole", then it just kinda went all quiet. He opened his eyes. The guys were gone, there was no one driving, where the hell was he, what were all these tall trees either side of the vehicle, a Forest ? and what were these Chinese lanterns doing in the car where the guys had been sitting, they had a ssssssstrange gggggglow about them, kind of orange but not clockwork orange. "Brutus", strange orange light, "Brutus", orange, very bright orange "Brutus", "what is it" shouted Brutus. "I'm very disappointed in you Brutus", "what, who's there" said Brutus, "It's me in the radio, Pete Tong" said Pete Tong, "I am really most upset by this whole affair, you have let your fellow colleagues down very badly they were relying on you to help them through the opening & closing routines & carwash in the middle, the 1970's version on the EMI label with Hamster toggles in the mix", "I'll be alright Pete" said Brutus, "I've got some T5s to see me through the evening, I'll be shipshape in no time at all", "T5s young man, why didn't you say so in the first place" said Pete, "I've got ultimate orange as well Pete, listen Pete mate, sorry to let you down, I listen to your Essential Collection, ah mean Selection every week mate, it's the dog bollox Pete, the Chaeta's Cvnt and don't you worry about that time at the Tunnel Nightclub Pete when you couldn't work the f***ing mixer Pete and you had to get Tevendale to play your choons for you, you A list DJ wanker you know ah mean that happens all the time with DJs like Boy George & You"............

"Brutus,Brutus,Brutus", who are you talking too ? asked Levi, shaking Brutus furiously. "What, What" said Brutus. He opened his eyes, the lanterns & the tall trees were gone & the guys were back. Two in the front glaring at him in the rear view mirror & Levi still shaking him. "Guys when did you come back" asked Brutus excitedly. "Eh" said Levi, "I've got Dave on the CB radio", "Ten-four toilet duck" said Brutus on the handset, "Shut yer hole" retorted Dave on the handset, "your a fanny" said Dave, "Oh shut up Dave, I've just had Pete Thong giving me a hard time as well, I'm really sorry, I'll be fine, I've got pro plus from the chemist, it'll be ok, don't tell Mark ya wee arse licker", "Don't tell Mark" retorted Dave, he won't have to be a rocket scientist man, he'll have one look at your eyeballs & your first gig could be yer last", "anyway I've got Glove here wanting to talk to you", "ten-four toilet d", "shut it you" said Gloves "your a fanny".

The atmosphere in the lead car was far more amiable. Mark was day-dreaming, they had left the suburban brawl of the inner-cities & were nearing Stirling. They had just swung onto the major roundabout with the services & were taking the Bannockburn junction, the hills & trees & greenery everywhere swung up in front of him. It was a glorious sight compared to the high rises & smoking & belching of Glasgow.. Stirling castle loomed up ahead like some sort of medieval time warp. The Wallace Monument loomed ahead also, overlooking the Sword Hotel, where the Highlanders were to return in years to come to ply their wares to the fair maidens or damsels in distress. William Wallace would have turned in his grave if he could see what the guys were getting up to at the feet of his memorial. Or maybe he would have just smiled & thought to himself, so that's what "freedoms" all about eh ? Mark was feeling pretty damn pleased with himself. He was glad that he had employed the services of the two veteran strippers Detox & Ramsbottom. They were both still shit hot at entertaining a crowd & were still top of their game. Detox had been in the game for ten years & pretty much new all he had to about the garment removing game. His speciality was the Officer & Gentleman outfit, with his dark looks & tight body, the white naval uniform looked very impressive on him. He was from Glasgow, Socks & Hero had already worked with him & most definitely rated him. Ramsbottom was English from the south of London & interestingly enough his speciality was the full kilt outfit, clan old style, with the Jacobean shirt & tartan sash. The icing on the cake though was the sword. A full length f***er but with blunted down edges. He would do the whole traditional kid on sword fight number & visually it was very impressive, especially if there was a good spotlight in the venue & all the lights would be dimmed. Mark just shat it every time he swung it around his head though, he could visualise heads getting lopped of. "That's us nearly there" said Marty as they pulled away from Greenland back into Greyland. The High St opened up in front of them, they could see the big neon Mecca sign up ahead. Dog & Mark took a deep breath at the same time as the first night nerves came rushing back.

We were met by the Manager & a couple of his staff & ushered through the labyrinth of corridors to the changing room at the back of the stage. The Manager was in a great mood, the house was packed, but there would be nobody shouting house tonight. Well at least not after the next hour. A game was in session at the moment and the eyes were down. All was quiet apart from a dude on the mic sounding like a demented android reading out the numbers "one and seven, seventeen", God how much sometimes must he just want to shout out "I wear a dress when I'm rogering yer Daugher Agnes har har". Detox & Ramsbottom were already there. It was going to be a busy & sweaty changing room, seven bloody strippers getting ready. Dave busied himself finding out what music D & R required, Marty & Mark disappeared with the manager to check out the lights & stage situation & talk business. Gloves started bringing through all the PA gear. "Gloves, fancy a hand" said Levi, "Yeah cheers Levi" replied Gloves,"F*** off" laughed Levi. Gloves wandered of grumbling away to himself. "Hey Dog, Brutus got full of E & Jellies last night at the Subbie & is going to F**** up all the group routines" said Socks. "You're a fanny Brutus" replied Dog. Brutus didn't reply just looked dismal and went and lay down on the floor. The guys apart from Brutus went to have a peek through the stage curtains. "Jesus" whispered Hero, it's f***ing jumping. He was right there was hardly an empty seat in the house, they still all had there heads bowed, like worshipers at a Church on a Sunday, while the Minister lead them in prayer. "One and three, unlucky for some thirteen" the android Minister read out to His flock. There was quite a few blue & purple heads bowed to numbered knots & crosses Hymn books, but there was also a lot of young poontang. Dave's head poked out beside them. "Is there many short skirts" enquired Dave. The Android was just finishing up. "That's me ladies" his robotic voice reverberated around the massive room. "I believe the Highlanders have arrived & are backstage & are getting oiled up right now" the vocodered voice boomed out. The place erupted in cheers & hollering, the hymn books were thrown to the side. Silent worship was over, it was she-devils time again. The boabey worshiping hour had arrived & they were ready.

"Who wants some boabey" shouted Disco Dave into the mic. Cheers, foot stamping, shouting! "Well Boabey couldn't make it tonight" replied Dave. Laughing, booing, more foot stamping. "I'll take you through the rules of the show" shout Dave as he threw a bit of Tony de Vit's "Burning Up" through the speakers, shouting, clapping. He threw the fader back down to cut out Tony, "There are no rules", he threw the fader back up, "You got me burning up" screamed Tony, hollering, screaming, and shouting. He threw the fader back out, "If one of the guys pick you out" fader up, "burning up", fader out, "You've not got to get up" fader up "burning", fader out, "but if you do" fader up "up", "I'll guarantee you" fader up, "you got me burning up", fader out, "you'll have a good time", "so if you don't want to get up, just say no thanks or f*** off" fader up "burning up , burning up, you got me burning up". The guys were ready, they were bricking it though, nobody was saying anything, and they were just walking up and down nervously behind the curtain. "Don't make a cvnt of it Socks" said Hero, Socks just ignored him & continued taking deep breaths & striding up and down. The song before the song was just finishing, Dog peeked through the curtains, and he could see Mark & Marty at the very back of the room watching. That was the music, they lined up and swaggered onto the stage, the place erupted, the women were all out of there seats. The guys lined up with their back to the audience. Jesus they could hardly hear the music over the women screaming. It went well though, they were all in time & defo no major f**** ups. They all filed off, buzzing like they had never buzzed before, better than sex, better than drugs, what a f***ing buzz, world class said Hero. Detox was ready, He was dressed in leathers, on he went, and some cheesy yet obscure dance remix of Kylie Minogue, The place was going mental. The guys had warmed up well for him he thought to himself as he burst the first few moves. Brutus went back for a lie down, Mark came in, "Well done guys, that was electric" He said. "What's up with you Brutus", "Oh he's ok Mark" said Dog, "Just think the nerves got the better of him, he will be fine". Mark shrugged and left the room. Brutus gave Dog an appreciative nod & then closed his eyes again. Hero was next on, he had this mad 80's new romantic style outfit, with black trousers tapering down to a narrow ankle & a thick black belt, with a two tone double breasted shirt. He was on with a skip and a jump, "I'm too sexy for my shirt" roared Right said Fred, and he was right, although it should have been double breasted shirt.

Hero had some really, really tall bird wrapped around his waist & was carrying her onstage. Once onstage, he hoisted her up so that she was sitting on his shoulders, legs dangling down his back, crotch push right into his face, Hero had his hands on her bum supporting her & was lapping away at the front, like a cat at a plate of milk, she had on a short skirt & Hero's head was half way up it.

Socks was on next, after busting a few dance moves, he dragged a girl on stage & lay her on the floor, He then opened her legs & then pushed himself away from her by about three feet, he then dragged her ankles before pulling her into his face, his tongue out, her legs open, she was wearing jeans. Socks pulled himself up and done the splits over her face, his g-string settled on her mouth and nose and he rode away.

Then it was Levi, The girl was placed on a seat onstage, no arms on the seat, Levi, walked slowly around her, playing to both the audience & to her, removing his clothes slowly & seductively, upper body naked, torn faded jeans on with a silver Versace belt & black studded S & M straps on his arms. He straddled her & slowly grinded into her as Frankie goes to Hollywood told everybody to relax.

Dog decided that one female wasn't enough & brought two onstage. One on a chair at one side of the stage one on the other. The Brad Fidel soundtrack to Terminator 2 kicked in as his leather bound, water gun carrying character walked on stage & started pumping the women with sprays of hot, gushy water from his gun. Then removing his outer layer of cyber dine metal over liquid crystalised flesh, well his leather jacket.

Brutus entered the stage to "don't know much about history, don't know much about geometry" which was definitely true. The quilt was already on stage, he strolled over to it & after removing his cowboy style denim jacket, lay down slowly with his back on the quilt & slowly raised his hips in the air to undo his jeans & lower then over his cowboy boots. All the women stood up to get a better view of this guy stripping lying down.

Ramsbottom was on last to finish the first half of the show. He wielded his sword over his shoulder & strolled out to the strains of "Scotland the brave" , the English stripper all dressed in tartan. Mark & Marty were backstage with the guys, Gloves was running about sorting out the correct piles of clothes. "Guys that was fantastic" shouted Mark beaming, "You were absolutely fantastic". "Yeah I was, wasn't I" laughed Socks, "I don't know about the rest of these clowns". Everybody was buzzing even more than the open routine, apart from Brutus who was back to lying on the floor. "Even better than shagging Rachel Welch" said Dog, "How the f*** would you know ya fanny" laughed Hero. Detox walked out of the toilet & stood over Brutus, "I think you're in the wrong game son" He said, "You'll never last", Brutus just grunted and didn't even open his eyes. The guys all laughed again. They were happy, all the hard work had been worth it. The women were putty in their hands. There was nothing they could not handle now. They had broken their duck.

Five

"Last call for British Airways flight BA1265 to Fingerolla, leaving at gate 11, would passengers Dog, Hero, Socrates, Brutus & Levi please make their way to gate 11 immediately", The intercom buzzed & switched off. "Hero, you can get bloody cheap booze over there for Christ sake" said Socks, "It's the last bloody call, were going to miss the flight", "Ok, ok" moaned Hero. They left duty free & hurried in the direction of gate 11. A British Airways dude with a walkie talkie came hurriedly up to them. "Are you guys going to Fingerolla", "Yip, sorry, I had to drop my pregnant wife off at the hospital" said Levi, The guy just gave him a look, "run" he shouted at them, "the plane is waiting for you". The guys all picked up their feet & started to horse it towards the gate. "hup 2,3,4" shouted Brutus. They arrived at the check in desk and quickly got their tickets & passports checked. "Your late" said the girl on the desk, "His wife was pregnant & had to get dropped of at the hospital" said Socks pointing at Levi. They were hurried outside & went up the stairs onto the Jet, the stewardess at the top glared at them, "evening" said Hero. "Your really, really late, the plane has been waiting on you" She said, "His wife was pregnant & and we" Brutus cut himself short as he felt that a slap from the Stewardess was imminent. They all walked to the back of the plane to take their seats. The passengers were all glaring at them. Socks pointed to Hero, "It was his fault".

It was June 1995, the Highlanders had been booked for a two week mini tour of Spain incorporating Fingerolla, Calahonda (where they would be staying), Belimadina, Toremolinos & Porta Bennous. Mark had set up the deal with an agent based in Calahonda. The guy had been putting on acts for years on the Costa, Solo Singers, Bands, Comedians, DJs, Karaoke Presenters, Dancers & female strippers. This was the first time though that he had booked male strippers. He had shopped about, he had contacted half a dozen male dance troupes, The Dream Boys, The Men of Texas, The Ladykillers, Centaur, The Centuarians & The Highlanders. It was only the latter that had been reasonably affordable. He had known that the Chippendales were totally out of his budget. Even some of the other dance troupes were very expensive, they wanted fancy hotels, limo driven to the gigs, all their food free & a bar tab every night. He had managed to get the Highlanders without their Manager or DJ or some Road

Managers guy called Marty. He had hired a Villa a spit away from his apartment. He said he would get them a couple of beers, so a couple of beers it would be. They were to get their own grub, no way was he feeding these guys (he would rather keep them for a week than a fortnight), he was using a mate to drive them around, he had a small car hire company, so they would get some large sized vehicle to take them to gigs in the evening & maybe give them some small sized number to drive around during the day by themselves. He had to pay quite a large deposit before they went over to concrete the deal with their Manager, but he only had to pay them cash after every couple of gigs. He had struck up quite a sweet deal with the venues where he would take all the door money & they would get the bar. He was selling the tickets at a good price & they were mainly going like hot cakes. A couple of the smaller bars hadn't sold so well yet but they were later in the tour & he was confident that once the buzz picked up it would be fine. He had made some plans for PR on the Island and it was going to start almost immediately after the lads landed.

"Ladies & Gentlemen I will be starting the descent to Fingerolla shortly, please put your seats in the upright position & put your tray back into the locked position, once again may I take this opportunity to thank you for choosing to fly with British Airways & I hope you have had a pleasant flight " announced the Captain. "Pleasant flight" said Hero, "lodged in between you two fat bastards,I don't think so", "That's calling the kettle black that, isn't it" said Brutus. He looked across the aisle at Socks & Levi, they were both straining to get a better view of their new home for two weeks. The plane grounded to a halt, everybody done their usual & jumped up & opened the overhead lockers & removed their own personal piece of luggage & stood there like sheep and waited. Bleet Bleet. The Stewardess was saying goodbye to all the sheep, thank you, goodbye, thank you, bleet, goodbye, bleet. It was the lads turn, totally ignored. "Goodbye Gloria" said Levi, ignored. They followed the flock into the reclaim area. Immediately they noticed the increase in temperature. "Jesus" said Dog, "Am sweating like a rapist during a prison riot". All the sheep got their bags & all the Highlanders apart from Socks, he was standing with one sports bag containing half of his gig gear. His suit bag with a couple of outfits was missing & so was his personal sports bag with all his day to day clothes, toileteries etc. "Shit" said Socks, "I don't bloody believe it", "I'll have to go and find somebody". Socks headed off in the direction of where the rest of the sheep were going. "That's pish" said Dog, "off all the bloody trips we've been on & it has to happen on this one", then he suddenly ran up to the end of the conveyer belt & jumped on & stuck his head through the big rubber strips at the far end. "What's the fool doing" said Hero to Levi & Brutus. "Hoi" shouted Dog, "whose got Socks bags, ya greasy bastards", "Shit Brutus, get him out of there before we all get arrested" shouted Levi. Socks came wondering around the corner, "I've got a claim form, It'll take up to three days to get them back", "don't worry about it dude" said Hero, "we can all give you a few t-shirts & underwear & stuff", the Guys all laughed, "Yeah, and we've all got a spare outfit or two that you can use" said Levi, "So chill dude it will be fine". They all headed for passport control & then headed out into the main arrival area. There was a reasonably tall guy in his fifties with grey hair & specs, short sleaved stripey shirt on & light coloured trousers with a placard saying "The Highlanders". He was standing next to a woman in her mid forties, quite plain looking but with a youth that exceeded her years and a nice buxom figure to fortify it. She was wearing a light coloured blouse & a wrap around skirt & Jesus sandals. The Guys trotted over, "Sid & Nancy" said Hero, "welcome to Fingerolla guys" said Sid, yes this is my wife Nancy. "I trust you had a pleasant flight", "we nearly missed it & then Socks got a couple of missing bags" replied Brutus.

They all climbed into a seven seater mpv, which was just as well as there was seven of them. Swung out of the airport & onto the dual carriageway, heading into the main drag of Fingerolla & then towards Callahonda. The heat was intense & it was only June. They put down their windows & let the cool breeze fall over their faces, they closed their eyes & savoured the moment. The many billboards at the side of the roads advertised local pubs & clubs, pictures of fresh faced young men & women in skimpy outfits, bikinis, shorts, sunglasses, having fun, smiling, saying come here, it's the coolest place on earth, give us your money & in return you will meet the boy/ girl of your dreams & you will get your brains shagged out. Sid & Nancy were up front, well obviously Sid was driving. He shouted back to the guys, over the sounds of the wind rushing in through the open windows, the cars & trucks whizzing by beside them & the low murmur of some Spanish girl on the radio, "i've set up an interview with you on the radio, Radio Fingerolla, our local station, I am due to call in about twenty minutes, I just have to pull in further up ahead & we can do it over my mobile, is that ok", the Guys all murmured an approval. Jesus hows that for efficiency they had just bloody arrived. The mpv grinded to a halt up on a ridge overlooking the ocean about ten minutes later. It was a beautiful sight, the sparkling blue ocean spread out in front of them for as far as the eye could see, small white shapes bobbed up and down here and there all over the massive blue tapestry, one of the Gods farted and a ripple went over the cool, smooth surface. The sun was glaring down on them & they all immediately started sweating again now that the vehicle had stopped. "We'll get you guys a nice cold drink as soon as we arrive at the Villa" said Nancy, the Villa, that sounds good thought the Guys silently, "then we'll get you some food, you will only have a couple of hours after arriving before we have to set of again, back into Fingerolla for your first gig". Sid had phoned the radio station while Nancy had been talking & was chatting away to somebody in Spanish, "Bueno, mucho Bueno Miguel" said Sid, He turned to the Guys, "Ok, do you all want to take part or will it just be one person", "You do it Socks" said Dog, "Yeah ok" said Socks. Sid then said ok, one minute. They waited while Sid fidgeted about with the Radio so that all the Guys could hear the interview. He found the station & they could hear some DJ speaking in Spanish & every now and then Highlanders getting mentioned. Sid said ok into the mobile and then passed it to Socks. It was a first generation mobile, think of the mobile that Dom Jolly uses in Trigger Happy TV (I'M IN THE RESTUARANT NOW), and you will be close to this bad boy. "Hola" said Socks "Como estas", "Bueno, gracios", all the Guys sniggered in the back of the Mpv. "Welcome to Fingerolla" the DJ said over the Radio, "thank you" said Socks into the brick, "It's wonderful to be here", "Can you tell us a little about your dance troupe, where you are from, who you all are & where you are planning on working on the Island" said the voice over the radio, perfect English with the Spanish lilt, "certainly, we are called the Highlanders, it comprises five dancers who are, "Brutus T Goldsmith, Levi Action Slacks, Hero, Dog & myself Socrates, we are from Glasgow in Scotland & have been stripping for four years now. We shall be working in Fingerolla, Calahonda where we are staying & if anybody wants to come back for a party I'll get you the address later, the guys laughed, Sid frowned, Nancy giggled, we shall also be working in Belimadina, Toremolinos & Porta Bennous". The Dj went on to ask some more questions, some of which Socks did not know, so he passed the brick back to Sid to pass out dates & times & venues. He finished the interview & then drove on to Calahonda.

They arrived at 6pm, they would have to leave again at 8pm for the half hour drive back into Fingerolla. The Villa was superb, there was two side by side, they had the one on the left, it was pretty big, three bedrooms, a very spacious living room and a reasonably sized kitchen & bathroom. The most important thing was of course that it had a pool, the guys just stood for ages and stared at it. Totally still blue water, with sunbeds stacked up around the side ready for use. Nancy had already bought them some provisions & had busied herself making the guys some lemonade, they all took five miuntes to sit on the loungers & sip down the lemonade, it tasted great, why did sprite & lemonade always taste so much better abroad. "Come on" said Sid, "leave your bags at the moment, lets go eat, there's a great wee restaurant just around the corner & we can talk business at the same time". He was right the restaurant was great, it was quite quiet, just a few holidaymakers grabbing a bite before getting ready to go out for the evening. They all ordered pizzas apart from Nancy who just had a salad. The pizzas were the proper Italian thin crust style, a nice crispy base with ham & pineapple that just seemed to melt in your mouth. Sid explained about some of the plans he had for PR, getting the lads to go around the pubs wearing especially made Highlanders T-Shirts for the tour and hand out leaflets. Levi asked if there was any more money in it for them for doing it & the guys just glared at him. Sid said how about free food all day & drink & that seemed to do for Levi, he liked his grub & the mention of the fact it was free was enough to give him a semi. Sid requested that they restricted themselves to just a couple of beers during the day before gigs but that they would get a few free beers at the event & they could drink as much as they liked after it. He explained that the beer was cheap & was pretty good. San Miguel was the best shout & the guys all knew that beer. After talking business, they just sat for another fifteen minutes having small talk, drinking more lemonade. They asked Sid how he happened to come over to Spain. He explained that himself plus his business partner back in England, Peter, who we would meet shortly, as he was our official driver for the fortnight, had a small forecourt & sold mainly heavy (Beamers, Mercs) cars. They had got themselves into a bit of bother & had to leave the

Country, the guys just looked at each other and decided not to ask any more questions. They had an hour to get ready. Sorted then, quick splash in the pool, shower, changed, brush the tootles, do a shit, on with the smellies, Bobs yer Unkle, Jeannies yer Auntie.

Their door got chapped at 8pm on the dot. It was Peter, Sid's partner. He was quite a small guy dressed the exact same way as Sid, short sleeved shirt, fine stripes, pair of light coloured trousers, grey hair & a big red face, also a big red beak to go with it. This guy liked a drink. The guys wondered if he was safe to drive at the moment. Ah well, who wants to live for ever. He was a right character with a strong cockney accent. Socks said to Dog if you shut your eyes it could have been Michael Caine. "Awright ma Son". The Bags were fired into the mpv, same one as this afternoon. Peter explained that we were meeting Sid & Nancy at the gig. Some snooker club in Fingerolla. So we set off again, this time back the way we came. "Cooshty". Peter was a pretty knowledgeable chap actually, He went into great detail about the history of the Island & the long forgotten battles between Spain,France & England. He explained that there was still a lot of ruins on the Island from these times & that we should try and go and see them. Aye right, we'll crack the jokes, site seeing was not down on our itinerary list. We pulled up outside the Crucible Snooker club right in the centre of the main drag of Fingerolla at 8.35. It was still bloody roasting. Then we stepped inside the air conditioned club, yes ya dancer ! Then we were shown to our changing room, bloody roasting, no air conditioning, doh ! Socks was quite partial to a snooker club or even any pub/bar that had a pool table. He was drawn to them like a horse to water, not to actually play pool you understand, but to utilise the table in his routine. He would usually jump on top of it in his first spot to test it for safeness & the sturdy factor. He had jumped on a few dodgy ones in his day & thought that the legs were going to give like a long distance runner pushing that extra half mile that's just not there. Then in his second spot, some poor unsuspecting girl would get dragged on top of it while he simulated sex on top of her, usually with her legs dangling over the edge of the table.

The first gig was only about three quarters full, a good mixture of holiday makers, Germans, Swedes, Norwegians, Portugese & British. Les the DJ that Sid had brought over to work the Summer was to be their jock for the two weeks.

He was there with his wife Gloria & teenage daughter Sam. He was a shit hot personality jock with all the patter. He had been a disc jockey for ten years back in old Blighty & had worked the last two summers over on the Costa. The money was good, He was working at least five nights a week, sometimes the full seven. He would also double up as a karaoke presenter. He had a pretty good set of lungs on him but not as nice as Gloria. She was a lovely looking woman. Tall, slim & elegant. She was also quite tanned already haven't been there for four weeks already. Sam was also a very attractive young lady for fifteen & the guys thought that in three or four years time would turn into a right stunner. They couldn't work out what Gloria was doing with a wide boy like Les, although of course they never told him that. They liked him, it was always a bit worrying when they couldn't take Dave with them to gigs as he knew the show inside out. It would be a problem if they were there for two weeks & the DJ was pants. Les liked the guys as well, he had been worried about a few things, firstly that they would be a bunch of fannies, especially when he was there with his wife & daughter & secondly that the would not accept him for some reason, he was worried that they might have ego's the size of their torso's. He had been wrong, they were a total laugh & nutters but in a good way. They were totally down to earth & had absolutely no airs & graces about them at all. He knew that over the next two weeks they would become close friends & have some great memorable times together.

The first gig went without problem, everything ran smoothly. Especially their sweat, that ran smoothly down their faces & ran onto their pecs & then bounced onto the floor. Jesus it was hot, damn hot which is fine if your with a women but not if your stuck in the middle of a snooker club in Fingerolla. The five of us walked off after the end of the finale, Robert Palmer had taken us through "Addicted to love" one more time, we certainly seemed to be addicted to love the number of times we had busted a few moves to that routine. Hero & Dog were ready first, over the coming two weeks Hero & Dog would always be bloody ready first. You see their philosophy was that the first ready gets the first choice of the spoils from war, in this case Poontang. You couldn't really blame them I suppose, it wasn't every month that we get invited over to Spain to ply our wares & there was some fine top quality totty over here. I suppose back home we are used to Scottish birds week in week out, not that there is anything wrong with that. I have always said that when you are walking down Argyle St on a Saturday afternoon you will see some fine, fine sites, but this was Spain & the number of darlings over here on holiday was exceptional & after all you only lived once. Saying that though I still felt that they were sad bastards, there would be plenty for everybody. Just play it cool, or as cool as you can get in the bloody sweltering heat. Hero & Dog had disappeared; they had got dressed & went sniffing into the main room. Socks, Levi & Brutus had gone through to join Sid, Nancy & Peter. Les was still firing on the choons, He had another thirty minutes left to play & Gloria & Sam were up dancing together. Les told the club owners that Sam was seventeen, which still wasn't old enough to be in pubs & clubs, but as long as he promised that she would only drink soft drinks then it wasn't a problem. She didn't want to drink anyway, she was a smart young lady & her dad didn't have to lecture her. She loved being over here, but her mum covered her eyes when the Strippers done the simulation stuff. Sid was delighted with the way the first gig had gone & invited the guys back to his place for drinks & a bite to eat. They had to wait of course until Hero & Dog came back, they claimed that the two Swedish birds had invited them back to their hotel which was just around the corner. They had smiles on their faces like Cheshire cats & claimed they had got up to a bit of jiggery pockery, the others thought that they were full of shit though, if they were telling the truth though they were lucky bar stewards as the girls were both darlings. It felt good getting driven back to Calahonda, the breeze was in their face again & it was getting cooler. I suppose we were relieved that the first night had went well, we would have felt bad, not so much for ourselves but for Sid, after all the effort he had went to. They got back to Sid & Nancy's apartment, which was only five minutes walk from their Villa. It was a nice spacious apartment two floors up & overlooked the swimming pool on one side which was shared by four or five apartment blocks inter-twined in the same area. The other side looked onto a construction site, a hotel was getting built but was a long way of completion. They sat up to the small hours of the morning talking & laughing sipping on big jugs of sangria. It was good to be away from home.

Six

It was about 2pm, the sun was still high in the sky & the tourists were passing by on the street. You can tell the ones that were from Britain & hadn't been there long without fail. They were the ones that were in either two categories, one, white as milk but covered up to the max, still wearing jeans as if they were walking down the High st in Glasgow, t-shirts on but with a wee betty jumper wrapped around the waist or a jacket if you were a guy. Trainers, white, white socks, with a baseball cap and factor two thousand sun block cream. Two, pair of shorts, flip flops & a football top on, no baseball cap & no sunblock, because your too f***ing stupid. Either white, or a scary shade of red because you've been burnt to a frazzle, but to f***ing stupid again to stay inside out of the mid-day sun. The guys were sitting in their favourite pub in Fingerolla, the Saloon. It was bang smack in the middle of the main drag & was a top vantage point for checking out the totty as it strolled past. They were four days into the tour & were starting to feel pretty relaxed, the San Miguel & Sangria was assisting with that task also. They were at their favourite table, outside on the side street but under shade from the canopy. A train on wheels passed by on the street outside dragging about thirty sightseers along in its small cramped carriages. "Hey, Hey,Hey" shouted the Strippers & clapped loudly as the choo choo drove by. The driver gave them a wave & clapped back. Hero had done this on the second day there & now we all done it. Don't ask me why it was just something we done. A group of Spanish & Mexican Girls walked by on the sidewalk. "Hola ce tu cia" shouted out Brutus at the girls, the guys all shouted "ce tu cia", some Spanish Girl at a gig told us this meant "sit on my knee", but it could mean bloody anything, but the guys loved it & used it at any given opportunity when a bit of skirt walked by. I suppose it was politer than a wolf whistle, but not by much. The girls just giggled & waved at us & kept walking. Sometimes they would stop & try and converse with us but the communication sketch proved to be a bit of a problem. Most of the time they just kept going. "Gracios senoritas", we would shout after them. They would shout something back, probably go shag a pole or something.

They had a bit of pr to do that particular afternoon. They were to wear the specially printed Highlander Tour 1995 t -

shirts & go around bars & restaurants in Belimadina, where they were to be working that night. Peter was picking them up at the bar any time now. They had had a late breakfast in the same cafe they had gone to that first night they arrived. They would do this pr sketch & then grab more grub before they had to get gigged up. It was a good laugh doing the pr, the t-shirts were quite cool & they just wore shorts & flip flops & bandanas on their nappers. We got to use "Hola ce tu cia" quite often, even with the English gals who seemed to quite like it although they didn't have a Scooby what we were talking about. It was hot work though & the lemonade was flowing later on. "So why should I come see you take clothes off" some Brazilian bird said to Dog, "Cause I've got a big cock" replied Dog. This line actually seemed to work with her, whereas back home you would just get a slap for that. She turned to her pals & they all took a flyer each, which also doubled as a discount voucher for the gig, you know, same price but you get two free drinks type deal. "Oooh are you Scotland, I luv Scotland, where in Scotland are you" enquired a very attractive Norwegian girl to Socks, "Glasgow" replied Socks, "have you been before", "slower please" retorted the Norwegian bird, "you speak fast" , "I know" said Socks, "I've got a lot to say & not enough time to say it in", "Slow please, slow", "Why I come to your show" said the Norwegian chick, "because Dog's got a big cock" laughed Socks, "A big clock" said the mystified Norwegian Girl, "Yes" replied Socks "He's got big hands and he likes to use them". "Socks just give her a flyer" shouted Peter, "we have to rock n roll", there's only time for another fifteen minutes.

"Whit sort of bloody name is Gina's Palace anyway" Levi asked Peter. They were in the mpv on the way to the Gig. "It sounds bloody gay", "Funny you should say that" laughed Peter. "Oh no" said Hero, "your joking aren't you", "well actually they do have gay nights quite often, but you will be glad to hear that tonight is not one of them, although there may be a few blokes in, I hope that is ok" replied Peter, "Naw it isn't ok actually" retorted Brutus in dismay, "No guys Peter" that was arranged before we came over, birds only, that's the deal". This was a major blow to the guys, they knew that blokes at a gig did not work, for various reasons, one, if females know that there is guys there watching them, then they don't let themselves go as much, it's a kind of tribal thing, when they are all women together, they connect, the whole sexual equality sketch is thrown out of the window, they don't care about trying to compete with men in any way, they just totally let their hair down & have the time of their life's without men looking on & tutting & judging. Two, if there are boyfriends or husbands in then this widens the goal posts even further, they most definitely cannot let their hair down & this may even have a domino effect to their friends accompanying them. Three, there's also the angle where the blokes may be charged up with drink & their macho side, edged on by their fanny mates can result in the strippers getting hurled with abuse."Poofs, gays, wanks, bunch of fannies", which translated into non-macho language, actually means "I say old chap, one is totally overcome with jealousy with the way you get these gorgeous ladies so wet". Anyways we weren't happy bunnies, we knew that we were in a different Continent at the time, so it wasn't like back home where we would have resolved the situation by saying to the venue organiser "If the blokes don't f*** off there will be no show tonight" or "you can shove yer gig up yer arse, we are spitting our massive dummies right out the pram & were going home". Now this angle would hardly wash in Spain, "Sid you can shove the gig up your arse, were going Home", "what back to Glasgow or the Villa like ?". No so we done what any self respecting part-time stripper with a job back in the golf factory, getting a lifetime chance to throw his bits about in Belimȧdina, would do. "Ok then Peter" said Hero, "that's not a problem, a few guys will not matter" as he glared at Brutus.

Larry was there to meet them, he was the co-owner of Gina's Palace, his partner Lesley was at the beauty therapist getting his eyebrows done, but he would be along later in the evening. It was quite a small gaff, fifty people would have filled the joint, but there was only thirty in but it still looked busy. It was a slightly older crowd that evening, in fact it was a lot older with the average punter being about forty. Obviously Gina's Palace was for the more mature individual. The guys didn't mind, the chicks still looked good. Mainly English with a few Irish birds in as well and some Swedes & Germans again. They were all tanned up to the max & more than half of them looked quite well off, what with expensive dresses & shoes & handbags to match. They looked like the country club types, you know, breakfast in bed with the silverware, down to the gym for a quick pump with Brad the personal Trainer & then back to Brad's apartment to get pumped, then down to the salon in the afternoon to get the boofong trimmed & the nails painted. Meet the girls for a late Lunch before going to the Country club in the evening to meet the Hubby and friends over a g & t or five. "Hoi Brutus", shouted Dog in the changing room, "Do you think Gina's Palace will have Gina G as their signature choon old cheesy toes". Brutus was known to like his cheesy dance choons & used Gina G's "ooow ah, just a little bit" for years in his routines. "Shut it ya fud" retorted Brutus, "Ooow ah just a little bit, a little bit more" laughed Dog. The show got underway, Les came into the dressing room, "Guys you've got your work cut out for you tonight, they are not exactly the most responsive crowd in the world, I am trying all my best patter & I have even sent Gloria & Sam up on the dancefloor to try and get them up dancing, but it's not happening", "great", said Socks, "an Edinburgh crowd". All the Guys moaned. An Edinburgh crowd meant that they would just sit back & be like "come on then, entertain me". Edinburgh gets a lot more choice in the entertainment stakes than Glasgow, which results in the Edinburgh punters being spoilt for choice on a night out. Don't get me wrong the guys have had some top nights working in Edinburgh, but they all agree that they have to work their arses of for it. The show kicked off & the guys could see that Les was right, it was bloody hard work. They had done the full first half & had hardly got a peep out of the crowd. "They are not interested in the dance moves" said Hero, "We are just going to have to get down deep & dirty". Deep & dirty meant that if you normally take one women up for floor simulation, then you would have to take up two at the same time or even three. They were just wanting a filth show. So the guys turned up the heat in the second half & it worked pretty well, the women got into it.

They had finished the show & were getting packed up when Larry the co-owner came into see them. Larry was in his mid-forties, had short peroxide blonde hair with a kind of tin tin flick at the front. He had on a Hawaii 5-0 shirt and a pair of Versace jeans. He was also sporting quite a cheeky pair of trendy Jesus sandals. He was also tanned up to the max. There was a frown on his perfectly tanned face though. He wasn't a happy chappy. "Guys I have got a problem", "none of you guys got the boabey oot & the women are looking for blood". Larry hadn't used the expression "the full monty" because that expression hadn't been born yet, well not to the every day public. You see it was only 1995 & The Full Monty movie came out a few years later. Strippers however did use that term & that was how the movie title came to be. You see back then the Highlanders didn't get their willies out, well not very often & usually only when asked. We would go to a gig & the organiser would ask Mark if the strippers were going "the full way". By 1995 this was getting more common. Although we still were not very comfortable doing it. I suppose when we just going as far as the g-string, we thought of ourselves as "dancers", you know a professional entertainer, but as soon as the boabey was out then you were just a "sleazy stripper". I suppose prostitutes have the same kind of distinctions. If they just give out blow-jobs rather than the full nine yards, then maybe their not actually pro's just kind of good time girls getting a bit of cash on the side.

"I'm not getting my dick out" retorted Hero to Larry, "no way". "Neither am I" said Brutus."Listen guys" said Larry, "all I need is for one of you to do it, that's all, just so that they can go home saying that they seen a cock". "Well you get yours out then Larry" said Dog,"they all look the same you know". "How much does the guy get that's getting it out" said Levi. "How much" retorted Larry, "nothing, that's how much", "I have a fee agreed with Sid & that's all I am paying". "Ok see ya then" said Levi, "It's just that I would do it for £50, but if your not willing to pay, then goodnight". Levi started picking up his bags. "Ok ok ok" replied Larry "Ok i'll give you £50". "Go get ready". Larry left the room muttering away to the himself. Levi headed off to the bathroom to "prepare himself". The show drew to a close for second time that night.

Socks was outside when one of the the audience came up to him "Hi", "it's Socrates isn't it", "sure is" replied Socks, "did you enjoy the show", "I loved it, my name is Wendy", "did you enjoy doing the show", "yes the crowd was great & very receptive to the routines, thank you very much". "Where is the other Guy, Levi" said Wendy, "my friend Debbie really liked him". "He is just getting ready, he'll just be a couple of minutes", replied Socks. "Would Levi & you like to come back to our hotel for a drink" offered Wendy. "Well I would, that is very kind of you to offer, I'll just go and ask Levi, just give me a minute".

"Dude, there is a couple of older Birds out there asking us back to their hotel for tea & scones" Socks said to Levi. "Are you up for it", "what are they like" replied Levi, "well the one that is into me is ok, I've not seen the other one yet". Levi & Socks came out to find Wendy & Debbie sitting in a taxi waiting. "Well boys" shouted the other women who must have been Debbie, "are you coming". It was 2.45am, Socks was in the bedroom with Wendy & Levi was in the other bedroom with Debbie. Socks was thinking to himself, remind me to check out the older tottie more often, this old bird really knows what she is doing in the sack, what have I been doing all these years. There was knock at the door & Socks could here Levi whispering "Socks, Socks". Socks answered the door, "do you have any spare condoms, I only had one". Socks went rustling in his wallet & gave Levi a condom, "now piss of and don't bother me again", said Socks. He went back to snuggle up to Wendy. "Wendy I hoped you don't mind me asking, but how old are you", "Don't you know that a gentleman should never enquire after a ladies age", "Yes" replied Socks, "but something tells me that your no lady & I am definitely not a gentleman". Wendy laughed, "you cheeky bugger, I am forty-five years young", "Jesus" said Socks, "Your the oldest bird I have ever been with", Wendy laughed again. "Why thank you for saying Socrates". "Debbie and me are both divorcees & have both just managed to get our well deserved money from our philandering husbands", Socks shivered & through male bonding possibly felt sorry for the husbands for a moment. Wendy and Debbie were both from South London & were over on the Costa in search of a house, that they were going to buy & live in together. How the other half lives Socks was thinking to himself when the door got knocked again "Socks, Socks" Levi was whispering again at the door. "Levi why are you whispering, it is not as if we are trying to get a good nights rest or something", "Do you have any more condoms" enquired Levi, "what are you f**king doing with them dude, eating them". Socks was just jealous because he knew that he was a one shot wonder.

Levi & Socks got back to Calahonda about 8.30am. They (i.e. the Highlanders) had been kicked out the Villa by Sid because they kept disturbing the family next door by playing loud music & then when there had been a water shortage, having a bath in the swimming pool using soap & shampoo. The final straw was probably when Hero shagged one of the Bar girls from a gig in the pool. So we were all staying in Sids apartment know. Levi & Socks had no key, so we just grabbed a couple of sun loungers & crashed out in our gear from the night before, black jeans & black t-shirts. We must have looked some sight sleeping there when at the back of ten, bodies started appearing beside us settling down for a hard day by the pool. "Looked what the cat dragged in" commented Dog standing over Levi & Socks. He was standing there with Brutus & Hero. "What happened to the crochet twins" said Brutus, "very funny" laughed Levi, "were they away to the hairdressers to get their blue rinse in" said Hero. All the guys laughed.

The rest of the holiday (working) just seemed to fly by, it wasn't without incident, there was the rental car given to them by Sid that they destroyed. There was the day that the crochet twins came around on their bikes trying to find Levi & Socks as they hid behind a bush. Debbie actually came over to Glasgow at some point in time months later, trying to meet up with Levi. Wendy didn't try and do likewise with Socks, the Guys just told him it was because he was a duff ride. There was the day that Hero, Socks & Levi got dressed up in all of Dogs & Brutus clothes to go out socialising just as Dog & Brutus came home & caught them & made them change back out of them. Then there was the time that Dog had got himself that nice looking Brazilian bird that we had met one day on the strip (as in the Town main st, not stripping) & taking her for a nice romantic meal for two, when Hero & Socks had stumbled pissed into the same restaurant & Dog had totally ignored both of them. Dog and Socks had crept into a room where Hero & a bird he had met were sleeping & skelped him as hard as they could on his ass. The girl had woken up and went "Hero, Hero there is some guys in the room". Socks had met a girl on the last night at a karaoke night & the guys had thrown packets of condoms at him as he was snogging her in the corner. Finally there was the time that Levi & Socks had got home earlier than the other guys & had crashed out. The other guys arrived back in the small hours with some girls that worked in a bar that we would go to socialise in after working. One of them we called "Saliva pants" which sounds very derogatory, but was because she wore leather trousers all the time & had a right high opinion of herself. Levi & Socks had agreed to go and crash out on the sun loungers so that the guys could have some privacy when Dog appeared out ten minutes later because Saliva Pants have given him a knock back. har har ! I am certain though that whatever happens to the Highlanders, wherever they may be in the world and whoever they may be with. that the two weeks in Spain in 1995 will stay in their memories forever.

Seven

"Hester, what are you doing", Linda screamed. "What's with the bloody Laura Ashley dress, where's your St Trinians", "I, I, I just don't feel comfortable Linda, It's ok for you, this is my 1st Hen night & you have all got great figures, I've got breasts like bee-stings", retorted Hester. "You've not got tits like bee-stings, I've told you before they are fine" replied Linda, "they are not fine, and don't use that word, they are breasts, they're like tunnocks tea cakes, according to all the guys at the bible meetings". "Don't listen to these fannies Hester" said Linda. "Linda, stop cursing, you know I don't like it, sometimes I think you just do it to wind me up". Libby walked into the room, "Wot's going on like bonnie lass", "why are you wearing that Laura Ashley dress", "Don't you start Libby, I've just been through it with Linda", "It's ok Hester, we know that you are finding this all a bit strange, Edinburgh can be a bit over bearing the first time you go to it, especially with you being a Vicars daughter an all", "It's just that you guys are so experienced at going out & getting dressed up and stuff & I just don't know why I let you talk me into it", "we talked you into it Hester because you never have any fun, all you do is go to a bible classes & help homeless people and stuff, not that that isn't a very worthy & honourable thing to do, it's just that you are thirty-five, all you do is hang about with old folk & the guys in the bible study class & your getting married in two weeks & we just want to give you a good send off babes, because we love you", said Linda.

"I know, I know you guys mean well, it's just that Edinburgh, well it's so big. I mean do we have to go and see these Male Strippers" said Hester, "Hester your hurting our feelings" said Nicole as she walked into the room. "We have went to a lot of bother setting this up for you & you will bloody well have a good time whether you like it or not", "don't curse" said Hester close to tears. "Oh for goodness sake, bloody, bloody, bloody" said Nicole. Hester just looked down at the floor, tears were filling up in her eyes and she looked totally miserable. "Right" said Libby, "come on girl, you can put the outfit on later", Nicole gave her a glare. "Let's go get your hair done, then we can grab a nice meal & a bottle or three of wine & then it's on with the St Trinians, don't worry you can borrow my padded bra & then we are getting into real party mode, OK", Hester kept staring at the floor but nodded her head in agreement. Libby & Nicole went back to their room in the B& B and Linda hurried about getting Hester presentable for going out. She did feel sorry for the girl, she had a very strict up-bringing & especially coming from Dunoon, they weren't exactly used to city life. Well Linda, Libby & Nicole were to a certain degree, as they would jump over on the Western Ferry and drive into Glasgow & go shopping & dining & have the odd night out, but going all the way to Edinburgh was an extra hour on the motorway & must have seemed like a pretty big deal to Hester who probably got off the Island about twice a year. Hester went into the bathroom to get ready, she didn't like changing in front of Linda, She was probably the most comfortable with Linda, that was why she asked to share the room with her but she still felt really self conscious. What did they mean I was going to see some bobby's, did they mean that a lot of the men in Edinburgh were called Bobby. She wondered what Alastair was getting up to now. His stag do was in Glasgow & he had said that the guys in the bible class were going to take him to the ten pin bowling place. He was so lucky she wished that she was going ten pin bowling rather than to see sleazy men taking of their garments. Uugh !

"Jesus Christ" said Nicole to Libby, "do you ever feel like having Hester as a friend is like having Carrie out of that horror movie as a friend", "Yes, well" said Libby at least Jean isn't quite as bad as Carrie's mother in the movie, not quite anyway". They both laughed. "Do you think she is still a virgin" asked Nicole. "Nicole, you always ask that" said Libby. Well before Alastair there was only Archiebald & I don't think so some how", they both laughed again. "Well one thing is for sure" said Nicole, "we are not going to forget this weekend in a hurry", "you can say that again" said Libby.

The hairdressers "Essentials" was only five minutes walk from the B & B, both Hester & Linda were getting their boothongs done. The hairdressers was busy & they sat in the reception area reading Take a Break magazine. There was an article on male strippers. "Oh look" said Linda, "there's the male dance troupe we are seeing tonight, the Highlanders". "They don't look as good as the Dream Boys" commented Hester, "I don't know" said Linda, "They look too kinda perfect, If you know what I mean", "The Highlanders look like your meat & potatoes type guys", "what rough & ready" said Hester laughing. Linda laughed as well, "Yeah I suppose so, these other guys look like they spend all day in front of the mirror, when would we manage to get into the bathroom" replied Linda. They both laughed again. "I suppose they do look kinda sexy in their kilts" commented Hester, "do you think they are true Scotsmen", "Hester McCready", Linda smirked "what would your Mother say". They both laughed again. It was good to see Hester getting into the swing of it thought Linda to herself, she was usually so uptight all the time. Linda stared at Hester as she poured over the article in Take a Break. She was quite small and dumpy, with a big bum & a flat chest, very plain looking but with definite potential in the facial area. The odd time she had seen her make an effort, she had turned out not to bad at all, infact she had a really nice mouth and smile with hazel brown eyes set amidst a pale complexion of too many bible classes & not enough fresh air, which was a shame coming from Dunoon, as one thing it had in plenty was fresh air. She had also been quite a sickly child, with every allergy you could think off. She was allergic to dust and feathers & couldn't eat any dairy produce or strawberries. A strawberry had nearly killed her once. Her trachea had swollen up and she had been unable to breath, she had passed out & it was only through the quick action of the paramedics that had managed to save her. She was the only child of Michael & Jean McCready & was there pride and joy. They wanted her & Alistair to take over the Church & their loyal Parish when they got too old to manage it anymore. That's if the Church of Scotland elders allowed it of course. There should not be any problem. Hester had been over to Serbia twice with the Church Mission & had done some wonderful work with survivors from the war. She had been to Croatia where she had been ambushed by Guerrillas along with other missionaries but had been released unharmed after forty eight hours. She was a very brave women, it was just when it came to love & romance & every day life with her friends that she was very shy & introverted. Linda got taken 1st to get a hairdo. Hester stared at her. Linda was about 5' 4" with a lovely figure & natural blonde hair & piercing green eyes, she was very attractive & men loved her. Hester was jealous of her looks, which sometimes surprised her as she was not a jealous person, not materialistic or even that interested in looks or her appearance. The girls had to drag her over to Gourock to the shops or moan at her to get her hair done. The thing about Linda was that she was such a lovely girl. She had absolutely no ego & was so down to earth, unlike other pretty girls who seemed so bitchy & shallow. The thing was that she knew that Alastair really liked

Linda, she didn't think that he fancied her, just really liked her, because she was such a beautiful person. In truth Alastair did fancy the pants right off Linda but was in Love with Hester & would never do anything to hurt her.

Nicole & Libby appeared at the hairdressers just as Hester was finishing. Linda had been done for ages and was sitting reading Hello magazine. "Girls you both look gorggggggeous" said Libby, "I know" laughed Linda. "Your soooo modest" commented Nicole. They all laughed. "Ok" said Linda, "C'mon, food". "Yeah" shouted Hester, "my favourite pastime". "Ok" said Nicole, "Libby and me have been busy restaurant hunting, while you two have been farting about", "there is loads of Italian restaurants in Edinburgh, and Indians, but for some reason very few Chinese", "who fancies what". "Indian" shouted Hester & Linda, "Italian" shouted Libby. "I tell you what" said Nicole. "It is Hester's Hen night". "Why don't we go to an Indian now & we can grab an Italian before we shoot of back home tomorrow". "Done deal" shouted Linda. The Indian restaurant was quiet, it had just gone 5pm & had just opened. It was very fancy, the chairs had gold painted wood over green padded cushioning. There was a picture of Ghandi on the wall behind where their table graced the middle of the restaurant. There were fancy lanterns on each table with burgundy strings hanging of them with gold beads dangling at the end, like a maggot on a fishing hook. Libby ordered a cuarf of house wine. Libby was the most brazen of the four, She was slightly smaller than Linda, about 5' 3" and had shoulder length peroxide blonde hair & a massive pair of boobs, they were 34 E's & used to be bigger but she had a breast reduction due to back problems. Everywhere she went, they were on show. Low cut tops, boob tubes, low necked dressed, t-shirts two sizes too small. She wore bright red lipstick & had bright red nail varnish to match. She loved to wind guys up. She had a test for guys, if she went on a date & caught them staring at her boobs more than once on the first date, then they were dumped. So as you could imagine she went on a lot of first dates. There was lot of guys out there though that were smart, they had their timing down to a t. They would hold eye contact & work out how long she would generally look away for before returning to full eye contact & they would sneak in a quick look. Libby was Manageress in a bookies in Dunoon & Nicole was the Assistant Manageress. Michael, Hester's dad, i.e. the Vicar would complain to Hester that her friends were in league with the Devil having such an occupation, but Hester would point out her father's odd flutter on the Grand National and said that he shouldn't judge as Lucifer was too busy in the big Cities to cast his eye over such a small community as Dunoon.

"C'mon girls let's get Hester into her St Trinians outfit" shouted Nicole. Nicole, Libby & Linda were all ready. They had on the white blouses, short black skirts, school tie (borrowed from the store where they worked), long black socks (with garters) and high heel black shoes which definitely looked out of place. They all had false freckles on applied with eye liner & silly bows in their hair. Linda was objecting to the bows after getting her hair done, but Nicole and Libby were having none of it. Hester had deliberately taken a longer skirt than the rest of the girls & thought that she was real smart doing that, but Libby had worked out that she might have tried that & had brought a replacement. "Noooo way" yelled Hester, "way" all three of them yelled back. So after much arguing & dummies getting spat out the pram, they were ready. They had been drinking another couple of bottles of wine while getting ready & were getting very relaxed. Linda dug out the learner plates to go on Hesters back & the potty to put the money in. Both Nicole & Libby had brought hockey sticks with them, borrowed from the local secondary school. With the understanding that if they lost them ,they replaced them. "Do you really think anywhere is going to let you in carrying hockey sticks" said Linda. Libby & Nicole both looked at each other & burst out laughing, they hadn't thought of that. So with hindsight they agreed to leave them in the B & B. "Saying that though, they might have come in handy fending out the Edinburgh guys if they get a bit fiesty" laughed Libby. "Girls, you look amazing" said Mrs Ramsbottom, the owner of the b & b. "Go and slay them". "Thanks" they all replied. They had reserved a table at the front of the venue which was about fifteen minutes away in the taxi.

"Hoi, your a legs Man, aren't you Dog, check out the pins on the St Trinians bird" shouted Brutus. He was peering through the curtains at the back of the stage & clocked Nicole coming back from the bar with the drinks. Dog rushed over just as the big pinned bird was passing the drinks around the table, She was having to bend down quite low as she was about 5' 10" and the table was very low. The skirt was riding up to the bottom of her bum cheeks. "Wow" commented Dog, "she's a darling". Indeed Nicole was a darling, she had the same attractive looks as Linda but with short dark hair which seemed to make her even taller than her 5' 10". Her skin was also naturally quite dark with light brown eyes. She had really unusual eyebrows which nearly met in the middle & was more of a male trait than on females but it kind off suited her. Her Legs went on forever but she had next to no boobs, which didn't make Hester feel quite so bad. "Guys, can one of you use the bride to be" said Marjory the Manageress of the hotel they were working in. They had done this hotel fairly frequently in Edinburgh. It had a large function suite on the in the basement area of the hotel. There was a long bar running along the entrance to the function suite on the right hand side. A load of chairs and tables across from it & then a dance floor after the bar with more tables & chairs facing it. The changing room was right at the end of the function suite. "What's she like" asked Levi to Marjory. "She's no braw" replied Brutus. "She's the wee dumpy bird who looks like she wouldn't say boo to a ghost". "Let Hero get the tall one with the pins up" said Socks, She's perfect for hoisting onto your shoulders"."Very funny" retorted Hero. "Is there not a wee skinny one at the table". "Naw" replied Marjory. "Now who is going to get the bride up, or are you not wanting paid tonight".

"Check out the local birds" Libby said to Nicole, "their a right bunch of tarts", "that's the pot calling the kettle black, is it not Libby" commented Hester. "Why Hester, you little witch" laughed Libby. "Hardly", said Hester, "Now Libby you should know that I am on good terms with the Almightily, I am more likely to be an Angel or maybe even a Saint". "More like a fallen Angel" laughed Linda. "Linda, I thought you were on my side" slurred Hester. "I am darling, I am" replied Linda. "It's just that maybe this is not the right evening for comparing yourself to an Angel". "Why not" slurred back Hester. "Well darling" said Nicole, "it's just that you might get a boabey or two thrust in your face". "Right ok I have just about had enough of this, who is this Bobby character" said Hester "and why is he coming to my hen night", "I certainly hope you are not expecting me to dance with him or I especially hope you are not talking about something worse, there is no way I am kissing him. No,no,no. I will not be kissing a total stranger". All the Girls had tears falling down their faces. "Oh Hester, you are one in a million", commented Linda, "don't ever change baby". "Now look what you've went and done" said Libby, "I'll have to go to the bathroom to reapply my makeup". "Me too" said Nicole, "and me" said Linda. Marjory waited until all three girls had gone into the toilet &

then took that as her queue to follow them in. "Ok girls I've got the bride all set up, one of the guys is going to use her in the first half of the show & a different guy is going to use her in the second half".

"Oooow, check out the pecs on that guy" Libby shouted over to Nicole. "I know" laughed Nicole, "do you think his willie is as big", they both sniggered away. Hero strode up to Hester & and offered her his hand. "No way" shouted Hester, "go away, go away, I'm engaged you know", "No shit" replied Hero "I would have never have guessed, now move". Hero grabbed her around the waist & hoisted her over his shoulders in a firemans lift. When in the middle of the dancefloor. He hoisted her two legs open & placed her crotch in his face, while she faced over his shoulders looking at her three pals pissing themselves with laughter. Hero was lapping away like a dog between the sides of her short skirt & Hester was squealing. When Hero took her back to her seat she took a big drink of her Bacardi Breezer, but she was laughing. "That's was great fun" she said to the girls, "can I do it again". "Shit man, she was bloody heavy" complained Hero back in the dressing room. "What colour of pants was she wearing" enquired Levi. "Hester, your face was a total picture" said Linda. "What about the guy in the army outfit" said Libby, "He's mine, so you bitches keep your eyes & more importantly your hands off him". Socks had placed two chairs on either side of the dance floor & had put Hester in one chair & another girl from the back with a mad jumpsuit on the other one. He kept pushing their legs apart and thrusting himself into them. Then he would throw his legs over the back of their necks/shoulders & push his hands on the ground while thrusting again into their faces from behind. Hester was back in her seat "that was lovely" she said, "He had nice firm buttocks". The girls all laughed, Hester was getting very very drunk. "Ok" said Linda, "I would say mission accomplished, lets go back to the B & B before Hester passes out". "You guys go back" said Libby, "I'll see you later, I've got plans of my own, don't wait up for me". "Oh Libby your such a tart" shouted Nicole, "takes one to know one" said Libby, "anyway your just jealous". Linda and Nicole got Hester outside & she promptly threw up. Then they staggered of to try and find a taxi. The silhouette of Edinburgh Castle loomed in the distance. It's creepy exterior casting shadows on the ground. Its battle mounts standing like a ferocious sea in a storm, rising up into the skyline & reminding Edinburgh's inhabitants of it's murky & violent past.

Eight

"BELFAST", "BELFAST", yelled Socrates Mum. "I'm not happy about that Son". "Mum, the troubles have been over for six Years or more" replied Socks. "I don't care, you still hear about the odd scuffle from time to time" replied Mrs Socrates. "Mum, it will be fine, don't worry about it". What Socks was doing though was worrying. None of the guys had been to Belfast before & were all a bit nervous about it. Not that there was any real reason to be. As he had stated to his Mother, the troubles had been over for six years. The thing was though that they were going over to work for the agent who was, well, quite high up in the UDA. Not only that they had three confirmed gigs, Omah army barracks, some proddy team who were like a 1st division club in Ireland, their supporters club & some right UDA dodgy bar somewhere. So yeah smashin, it all sounded right safe as houses. Not just that, they were going at the time of a Bobby Sands memorial march & a major orange walk. Socks decided to definitely not tell his Mother these particular details.

It had been a strange old time in the Highlanders of late. They had fired Mark for ripping it into them on the money front. They had found out that Mark had been charging a much higher fee for most of the gigs than he had been telling the Guys about. i.e. he might have told them that a full show in and around the Glasgow area was £500 but intelligence had it that he was actually charging up to a grand on some occasions. So we had it out with him but he flatly denied it. We couldn't trust him anymore though, anyway that wasn't all, there had been a catalogue of events leading up to this point. Turning up for gigs and employees not knowing anything about it, arguments over unpaid money, no money for petrol, favouritism over who was getting one man & two man shows. Lots of lies. So the Highlanders had had enough, so Mark got bumped & we found ourselves a new Manager, a chick Manager. Patricia Longworth, or Trish for short. Trish had her own entertainment agency, PLC Entertainments. PL for Patricia Longworth & C for Carrick, which was her husbands surname, David Carrick. Seemingly he was the money behind the partnership & had financed the setting up of the agency for her. She had about thirty bands on her books, ten solo singers, five comedians, three karaoke presenters, two personality Dj's & now a male dance troupe. It was partly Marks fault that we ended up with Trish, as we had met her at a showcase. A showcase is an event that an agent organises to advertise & promote his or her acts to other agents & pub/club owners. We had met Trish at one of these events organised by one of Marks old friends and agents Jack MacKay. We had met Jack a few times & he was a right colourful character. He was always very smart, nicely turned out, silk suits & he always wore these stupid looking Disney ties that were all the rage in the mid-nineties. He found us an unruly bunch, probably because we were an unruly bunch. He was up to high doe that night, well understandable I suppose, it being his showcase. We were to do two routines, both group, no individual routines. Both the starting and closing routines. Both Mark & Jack wanted to sell us as unit, as a combined act. These things rarely go to plan and this was no exception. There was a problem with the music. Dave had been asked to do the music for the full night & he was having kittens trying to organise the various acts that were there that night.

"Bollocks to this bullshit", Dave shouted at Mark. "calm down Dave" replied Mark. "Calm down, f**k all, you can sook ma phat one" replied Dave, which really wasn't the best of things to be saying to Mark in case he took you up on the offer. "See all these f**kin prema-donna Mutherf**kas band assholes, they all think that they are Fake That" (we called Take That, Fake that, just because their music was by the numbers, cheesy, twat, shite). All the guys laughed, we were used to Dave losing the plot. If he didn't, well !! He just wouldn't be Dave. "I'll deal with it" retorted Mark, being diplomatic, "what appears to be the problem". While all this was happening, Jack was trying to greet all the guests arriving, doing the hostess with the mostess & dually trying to find out who was going on when. What made matters ten times worse was that The Highlanders who were due on in twenty minutes hadn't even unpacked their gear, infact Hero had just arrived five minutes ago. Jack had came into the room & had gone spare. He was cursing and shouting at us, now this would normally have two reactions, one, he would be told to shove his showcase where the sun doesn't shine or two, he would just be blanked as we went about our usual routine. On this occasion though it was Levi who decided to reply to the abuse, "listen Jack Macuntdan, shut yer hole". "Macuntdan" was Levi's interpretation of MacKay. We actually all thought that it was very creative of Him. So it stuck, Jack would always be Jack Macuntdan until the last Highlander alive drew his last breath. When the Highlanders were all Grandfathers & old men, they would sit with their grandchildren & tell them of their days as male strippers & Jack Macuntdan. "Levi, pack up your stuff and go home" Jack said. "F**k you Macuntdan". Jacks face went bright red, it was the colour of the old hermits face on his Disney tie. You could just imagine the steam escaping from his ears. "Levi, I will not stand for this type of behaviour at my venue", He sounded like a primary school teacher now, ticking of one of his young pupils. Levi walked up to Jack & squared up to him. Mark just stood there looking a bit forlorn & all the guys stood & watched and waited with baited breath. "Mark, where did you put the f**kin mic", Dave shouted as he rushed into the room. "Whits going on", he asked as the situation at hand shook him out of his current mental state. Socks decided that this was good time to intervene. "Levi, come on Bro, he's not worth it, lets get ready, c'mon man", Socks grabbed Levi by the arm & pulled him away from Jack. "You've got ten minutes" shouted Jack at anybody that was listening. He then stomped out of the room, not more than a little relieved at Socks saving the day.

Well Trish had been one of the agents at the Showcase & was more than a little impressed with the Highlanders. She then managed to get them a fair amount of work & always turned up at their gigs looking like a million dollars. She would wear an expensive business suit. She was one of the first people the guys knew to own a mobile phone when they first came out & always strutted around with her filofax, like a female posh version of Del Boy out Only Fools & Horses. When things went pear shaped with Mark, the guys had asked to have a meeting with her and had been to her house in Lanark a few times & also a few hotel get togethers.

Trish had set up the deal with Paul Macleod the agent in Belfast. She had managed to get a deal to bring the fully contained show to Belfast, including Dave & Gloves & herself. Paul would provide the PA equipment & DJ Gear. Dave would just have to bring headphones, mic & his cds. She had kept the costs down to agree to travel by sea & also stay in a b & b rather than a hotel. The guys didn't care, as far as they were concerned, it was a chance to go to another Country, and looked at the trip as a jolly. Which in essence is the correct outlook. Who wouldn't give the chance to travel somewhere to get paid for something they love doing & meet interesting new people.

"Where the f**k is Hero" moaned Brutus, "we have got two hours to get to Stranraer to get the ferry, It's Friday afternoon rush hour traffic & there is no sign of the big lump". We were all waiting on him at the WaterMill hotel again in Paisley. Trish was stridding up and down & was getting very impatient. She had already had a fallout with her hubby David over Belfast, he wasn't very happy with her going with us bunch of pervs, but she had put the foot down & things were a bit strained. The sound of Hero's Opel Manta could be heard over the sound of Trish's high heels cascading against the pavement, "Click click, clickety click", "Vrooom, vroom, click, Vroom, clickety vroom". "About time fudnuts" shouted Brutus at Hero as he came ripping into the carpark. "Right, are you guys ready yet" retorted Hero laughing. "Right, Dave & Gloves in Gloves car & the rest of you monkeys in mine" shouted Trish. Trish had a 320 coupe BMW but drove like Miss Daisy. "Trish shove over darlin" said Hero, "I'm driving". "Well ok" replied Trish, ever so hesitantly. Hero then proceeded to rip the arse right out of the motor. Trish was to sell the car when she got back from Belfast as, well, it just didn't feel quite right afterwards. Hero then proceeded to scare the pants off ever second motorist on the way to sunny Stranraer. Ben My Cree was waiting for them in Stranraer, this would be the boat that would take them to the land of Guinness, Magners cider & Leprechauns. Ben My Cree normally done the Heysham to Isle of Man run, but the normal boat was getting a few technical problems looked over. "Were all going on our summer holidays, our summer holidays" sang Socks. "Hey were going to Barbados" replied Levi. "Well I suppose Belfast does start with a B" replied Trish, "but it's hardly Barbados".

"How the hell does this thing float", commented Brutus as the guys leaned over the side of the boat. "Well you know" replied Socks, "It's to do with the overhead manifold gasket". This was Socks general reply to every technical question. "Nope" said Hero "actually I believe it has more to do with the twin carbine vollopter plopter chopters". The Guys all laughed. "Reallllllllyyyyyyy" said Dave "It was my understanding that the ballast tanks on both the starboard & port with the resonance chambers released h2o & oxygen at the correct levels so that the nitrate hamster toggles could revolve at the exact time required for the motion of the Boat with reference to wind direction & the sea conditions at any particular time", "listen to that guy laughed Gloves, "that's how to bullshit with style". "Nah" replied Socks "it's still the overhead manifold gasket". Dog came up onto the deck, "guys, guys, you will not believe this, they have an area called the quiet area, it's full of coffin dodgers"."So" replied Dave. "well I have this devilish plan". Ten minutes later Dog, Brutus, Hero, Socks, Dave & Gloves were all sitting two at a time side by side in the rather busy and very, very quiet "Quiet Lounge". Trish was far too embarrassed & more importantly mature so be involved with the guys childish pranks. She was beginning to think as Mark once did, why oh why did I get mixed up with these clowns. Well I suppose they did make her a reasonable amount of money & as much as she hated to admit it, she did have a soft spot for all of them. Anyway back to the Quiet Lounge, in amongst the sea of beige the guys had taken up position. The crusties were mainly either sleeping, reading or watching the black & white Fred Astaire, Ginger Rodgers movie. Dog started first with a really low and very long Snore "snoooooooooooooooooore", Levi picked up where Dog left off "snorrrrrrrrrrrrrrre", then Brutus "snoreeeeeeeeeeeeeeeeee", then Gloves. Until all Guys one at a time had their shot. Then when it went back to Dog's turn, they all snored at the same time. "Ding Dong" went the intercom, "Attention please, this is to act as a reminder that the quiet room is called the quiet room for a reason. If anybody wants to talk, laugh, shout, joke or snore loudly please make their way to other areas of the boat", "Ding Dong" closed the message on the intercom.

"Why do you think old folk wear beige all the time" asked Brutus as they all sat in the food eating area (where talking, laughing, shouting, joking & snoring loudly is generally accepted). "Cause of the overhead manifold gaskets" replied Socks. "Well it is funny you shoud ask that my dear boy" said Hero, "that is something that I have given long & painstaking thought on - NOT", "there is a perfectly rational reason" said Levi, "Littlewoods & Marks & Spencer's" use the same distributor. they are the only distributor in the world that make beige clothes for the OAPs". "Seemingly there was research done years ago and the conclusion was that it was mainly due to peer pressure that they would only wear beige or various colours of brown. This was due to the fact that they see other colours as rebellious, i.e. black or red is a defo no no, far too alternative & not keeping with the status quo at all. Not a British colour, oh no, not British at all. For instance you would never see Maggie Thatcher wearing black or red, well black if she was going to a funeral. White is also out, too young, too virgin, too wedding. Yellow, Green, blue, no chance, too bright, too alive. too not beige." continued Levi. "In fact the distributor that sells the clothes to Littlewoods & Marks & Spencers, they sell them to Littlewoods at a lower price than M & S. It's the exact same gear, it's just that the M & S punters are a bit posher & theoretically can afford to pay more. It's a bit like Tesco selling orange juice in their orange cardboard containers and then putting their value range orange juice in the clear plastic containers. It's the same orange juice at the end of the day. People just don't want to be seen buying too much of the value range because it makes them feel like peasants, but with the introduction of the self-service lanes this feeling of embarrassment will be reduced & mass buying of so said value products may ensue. To such an extent that Tesco & other supermarket giants may have to re-think the self service lane philosophy & only allow a maximum of say five value products per trip to the store, if you try and take more, a very loud embarrassing alarm goes off and everybody in the stores turns to look & point at you" finished Levi. "Levi" said Dog, "have I ever told you that you are a very strange & deep individual". "Even Dave would struggle coming up with such a bullshit story at such short notice" said Trish. "The worry thing is that he is able to produce such shit at the drop of a hat" said Socks. "No, no" retorted Levi, "I really have thought long & hard about the beige issue".

The Claymore B & B was a bit of a dump. Downtrodden, unkempt & had ringings of the house in the original Psycho movie with Anthony Perkins or the house in the Amityville Horror movie. The guys were two to a room & Trish had a room to herself. They had arrived at the port at 5.30pm & Paul Macleod the agent had met them. "A'right Lads" said Paul "Ah take eit use hid a gid Journey".

Note to the reader : you'll note that I rip the pish out of the Irish accent but not Scots. Well that's because I am Scots ya dafty.

Paul had a strong Northen Ireland accent which was strange seeing that he is from Northen Irleland. The guys took to him immediately, he was another colourful character. The lads had met quite a few on their travels but few as colourful as Paul. What is it about the Scots & the Irish that they just click ?? Is it because we are joined together by mutual understanding that wherever we go in the World nobody understands us ? or is it to do with the fact that we are both oppressed Nations & have fought together for hundreds of Years. Whatever the reason, Scottish guys love Irish birds, they could be the ugliest bit if skirt that you have ever layed your eyes on, but that accent, that bloody accent. Forget Helen of Troy who launched a thousand ships. The Irish accent could raise a thousand cocks. Imagine this, you're a Scots dude in Belfast getting down to do the wild thing with a Irish Bird that's fallen out of the ugly tree. You need some stimulation "Speak to me darlin", "Wot ya want me tae say fuckhied", "yeah that's it baby", "you've got the smallest cock i've ever seen ya beeg shoitheid", "Yeah baby, more, more".

It was 8pm and we were on our way to the first gig. The Highlander convoy was started by Paul in front with his Merc, then Trish with her Beemer & Gloves pulling up the rear with his Peugeot. Omagh army barracks was the first port of call. Socks rested his head against the backseat left hand windscreen of Trish's brief & took in the passing sights. The terrain was very similar to Scotland. As soon as you are out the big smoke, it is greenery everywhere & blue skies, well sometimes blue skies. Fields and fields rolled by. Thousand of trees pointing at the sky like rocket launchers (ok bad coin of phrase in Belfast). We rolled through quaint Irish villages where the chimneys poked out of the roofs like flower pots without flowers. Old men sat outside pubs smoking & drinking, the odd Burberry baseballed cap ned would appear wearing either Celtic or Rangers football tops. God, I can't escape it thought Socks to himself. Tractors would sit deserted in the middle of fields as if Armageddon had happened & everybody was either dead or roaming the countryside as flesh eating zombies. As they past through all of the Villages there would be barriers of steel resting against each side of the road. Seemingly this is for when there is orange walks. They can only go so far & stops the villagers from roaming into other areas & causing havoc. The Police of course would man the other side of the barrier ready for trouble. These barriers are very seldom used these days but remain as a reminder of the past. Small hedges at the side of the roads protecting the field like an army of soldiers standing at attention waiting on the next order. Cows & sheep grazing the grass. Tall Hedges, no cows or sheep, small hedges, cows & sheep back grazing, tall hedges, no cows. Eventually the convoy of three pull by a sign marked Omagh. Back into civilisation, office buildings, shops, garages, cars, people. They take a corner out of the main town area & head through a scheme of council houses. Lots of children playing in the street, single mothers pushing prams, a pub on every corner it seems. They take another corner & the barracks looms up before them. Barbed wire surrounds the complex at the top of tall fences. We pull up to the first security check station (there is two). A soldier sentry steps out of the security booth. Paul remains in his car as instructed by the sentry & passes over some kind of documentation. The barrier remains down. The soldier goes back into the booth & makes a call, checking the authenticity of the documents. The barrier raises & we move forward to a second barrier. This time a second soldier exits from the second booth with a long rod with a mirror attached to the end. He then proceeds to check under the car for a bomb or bombs. Paul gets the thumbs up & the second barrier raises & he proceeds up to a building where he is flagged down by a third soldier. The other two cars go through the same dance. First barrier, the papers that Paul had passed to each driver, second barrier, bomb check & then building with the final soldier. What was really surprising is that we did not get any body search & neither did our gear. Then again the troubles had been over a long time & everything was more relaxed now. I suppose also that they don't consider five strippers from Scotland to be the kind of threat that would fit into the bomber type category.

It was a bizarre gig. We had travelled by car all the way to Stranraer & then spent three hours in the ferry getting to Belfast to entertain a bunch of army wives & girlfriends from England & Scotland. You see the wives & gfs get to live in the soldiers quarters. The Irish still hate the army. So you are not going to find an Irish girl with a British Soldier. I am sure that it does happen, but most definitely not as a rule. We of course had not thought of that. Then there was the Staff Sergeant who fancied himself as a bit of a stripper & kept asking Socks if he could go onstage with him to do a duet. Well the guy seemed to be in charge & we thought it might have been very ignorant & bad for our health not to oblige. So Sarge & Socks went on to do a easily forgotten duet to finish the show. The Sarge of course went down a storm & only fell of the stage once, well he was rather pissed at the time. He then proceeded to shower us with drinks through in the bar. Poor Trish & Gloves couldn't get one as they were both driving. When it came to the point that we had to leave, we sneaked out without saying goodbye to Sarge as he wouldn't let us leave & kept insisting that we had one more. When eventually we did "escape" he ran after us until he ran out of steam as the cars headed towards the security gates.

Well that was Friday nights shenanigans

over. It was 11am on Saturday morning & we had just shovelled a late official Irish breakfast down our Gregory's. There isn't really much difference between an Irish breakie & a Scottish one or even an English one for that matter. The difference I suppose between English & Scottish is that the English one doesn't contain lorne sausage. You know that damn delicious square sausage that you can't get south of the border. You can't get a lorne sausage in Ireland either, their main difference is that you get that soda bread which is right tasty. Anyway we were on a mission once again. A quick shower, shave & a shit & Trish was dropping us of in Carrick Fergus for a bit of r & r. We had a mate there, well he was more of an uncle to us all. Jake was his name & hard drinking was his game. "I luv me drink" said with a strong Belfast accent. Jake was born & bred in Belfast, in his early forties & had lived in Carrick Fergus all his life. He would always tell us amazing stories about the two main opposing areas of Belfast. The Falls Rd (Catholic) & the Shankhill Rd (Protestant). We were to meet Jake at 12.30 in the Rangers supporters club in Carrick Fergus. We arrived about ten minutes early & headed straight to the bar. Brutus got all excited as he spotted that the bar was selling Budweiser on tap. "Ya f**king dancer" said Brutus. The club was busy as the Junior team was playing that fine Saturday & the locals were getting tanked up before the bus arrived to take them to the away game. So the bar was pretty busy as you could imagine. Brutus was having problems getting served, "hurry up ya fanny" shouted Dog, "I'm dying of thirst here". We had received a few strange looks when we arrived. Like these old western movies with the dude on the piano stop playing & the everybody stop talking, ok well it wasn't quite that bad but you get the idea. "Hey Mutherfukas, what you all staring at, who wants a piece of me, Eh ! well ! c'mon, come an get some if you think your hard enough" thought Socks to himself. He smiled, don't really think that will have went down to well. "C'mon to f**k Brutus" shouted Dog, "get the beers in ya total fanny". Nobody at the bar had approached Brutus, he was just getting ding'd. So in a manner unaccustomed to him he shouted "excuse me, six pints of Bud please", totally ignored. "Excuse me pal, 6 pints of bud please". it was as though he was the invisible man. "It's ok Danny, there with me", the guys all turned to see the beaming big red face of Jake hanging over their shoulders."Hey hey" shouted Levi, "Jake me old cocker spaniel, hows it going me old son" ? "Shoit" replied Jake "It's 12.30 in the efternoon & I've no had a dreenk yet".

The Guys all laughed. "Jesus Jake" said Dog, "what's the story with trying to get a drink in here", "aye well, there funny with strangers". So unfortunately we all got a little bit too relaxed. By the time we had finished in the Rangers supporters club we were pretty well on. Then Jake took us to another two or three watering holes. At seven o'clock we decided to get a taxi back to the B & B seeing that we were supposed to be at the gig for 8.30.

"Look at the fecking nick of him" screamed Trish pointing at Socks. "In fact look at the nick of all of you". "It's ok calm down Trish babe, we'll be fine" replied Levi. "No Levi you will not be fine, this may only be a pub gig tonight but it's sold out, so I suggest you all have a very quick cold shower each & I'll go and get the coffee", "what's more if you lot make an arse of it tonight & embarrass me, then your not getting paid & that is just for starters". "Take a chill pill the Trishster, its fine, we'll be fine...hic" said Brutus. "Hero my old Son" slobbered Socks, "I require some of your best T5's or some of that ultimate apple", "It's ultimate orange ya fud" replied Hero. "Don't worry Trish baby, I'm on the case, I'll sort him out in no time at all", "sort yourself out while your at it" sulked Trish as she stomped off to get the coffee. "Pphhhwww i'm totally shit-faced" said Socks. All the guys fell about laughing. "No way can you do this gig tonight boy" laughed Levi. "Shut it shandy boy" replied Socks. "What do you mean shandy boy" snorted Levi. "You know fine well what he means son" said Hero, "we aren't that stupid, we clocked you firing into the shandy's every time it was your round dafty". Forty-five minutes later we were all in the motors heading for gig number two. "Dave, how do you fancy a game of ping-pong" asked Socks. "Whit are you on about" asked Dave. "We just passed that ping-pong shop back there" said Socks. "Your havering boy" laughed Dave. "hahaha disco Dave, disco Dave" laughed Socks. "Oh no" said Dave shaking his head "your a nightmare". The pub was mobbed just as Trish had said. The guys were getting changed in the kitchen which had a door directly into the main area of the pub. They barely managed to hold the opening routine together but nobody really noticed, apart from Trish & Dave that is. They both stood there with their hands over their eyes. Hero was first out for his first individual spot, He walked out the kitchen door & straight into a pillar. He just seemed to bounce of it & kept going like nothing had happened. "Har har har" laughed Socks watching Hero through the window on the door. "Hero just walked into a pillar". Socks was soon to be laughing on the other side of his face (what does that saying mean ?), he went on next & fell on top of the girl he dragged up to use. Trish came into the kitchen at half time, "what the hell was that all about" ? she enquired. "Hero you walked into a pillar & Socks you fell on top of that fat bird you got up". "She wasn't fat" replied Socks, "just big boned". "Socks", Trish said Socks with such a threatening tone that he decided to shut up. "Yeah but we still smoked it" smirked Hero. Trish couldn't really argue, the Guys had went down a storm & the first half seemed to have straightened them out.

Sunday morning, Bobby Sands memorial March day. The Guys were not aware of this & had decided to go for a wee sorte around Belfast. As they entered the start of the Falls road they drove right into it. It was mobbed, there was hundreds involved in the March & there was twice as many walking along the road. "Just make sure when you drive along the Falls that you don't drift of the main drag into the schemes","not with a British number plate on your car","somebody might take a pot shot at your motor" Jakes words from the day before came tumbling back into the guys minds. There was some dude walking up & down the line of cars with a cloth bag taking donations. The guys decided that it would not be a good idea not to donate, so they dug deep & threw in some cash. There was murals everywhere, "Brits out", pictures of Balaclava clad militant soldiers. It was pretty scary. The guys tried to remind themselves that the troubles were long over. Everybody looked very sombre, Bobby Sands had not only been a local hero but a national legend to a lot of people. Margaret Thatcher's unwillingness to deal with terrorists & the hunger strikers especially had united a lot of the Irish people. Driving through these troubled streets or supposedly now peaceful streets, did kind of affect you. You did feel slightly ashamed to be British, then you remember the scores of young English & Scottish Soldiers that lost their life, not to mention the many innocent bystanders. There of course there was arguments for both sides, there are many stories of British brutality to the Irish people when they first took up home there. Then there was the family who were temporarily living in the same B & B as the guys who were from the Shankhill & had been threatened by the IRA & were forced to move out of their home. A husband and wife & two young children. As in any war, it is the children who are the victims.

The lads arrived home in one piece & busied themselves preparing for the final gig in the football supporters club that night. "Hey hey it's poontang city out there" laughed Dave. "You boys are getting a good send off tonight". "World classssss" smirked Hero. About six or seven girls burst into the changing room at half time. "Can I have photo of you guys" asked this rather attractive looking Irish lass, "You can have anything you want darlin" replied Brutus. "Is that right" chirped up a wee voluptuous brunette. "Does that go for all of us honey", "Yip everybody apart from you" injected Dog. "Oooh you cheeky monkey" replied the brunette. "I know what time it is" laughed Socks, "what time is it Socks" replied Hero, "its body-graph time". "What's body-graph time" another tall blonde injected. "Well Luv, I'll tell you" said Socks. "We take a magic marker & you provide us with a body part of your choice & we write on it". "write what" retorted the big blondeshell. "Levi was here" laughed Socks. "Shut-it you" frowned Levi. The guys always had a habit of signing the other guys names, just in case there was some comeback from green eyed husbands, boyfriends. Levi grabbed the big blonde by the hand & escorted her towards the ladies toilets. Dog done the same with the brunette. Dave just walked in time to see Hero & Socks both signing a couple of breasts. "I hate this job" laughed Hero. "So darlin" said Socks, "talk to me, say something", "like what" she replied. "Anything" said Socks, "anything at all".....

Nine

The mobile phone rang, Socks reached across to his bedside table & wearily answered it. "Hello", "yes hello, is that Socrates from the Highlanders male dance troupe" the voice asked. Socks scratched his eyes & rolled onto his back pulling the covers up to his head. "Yeah, what time is it" ?, "It's 11.30am" the voice replied. Socks had been working in Aberdeen the night before doing a one man gig & didn't get in until 3am & went to bed about 4.30am after stuffing his face & watching three quarters of a dvd. "Hello are you there" the voice enquired after Socks long pause. "Yeah yeah I am here, who is this". "My name is Hester McCready, would you rather I phoned back later, is this a bad time". "No it's fine Hester, how can I help you". "I was at a Highlander show three years ago in Edinburgh, you were passing out your business card at the end of the night & I took one". Socks brain started working overtime, had he fired into her, had he fired into her pal, did she have a baby & had now decided that Socks was the father & all her family had told her to contact me & threaten me with the CSA. I've got to stop watching Trisha & Jerry Springer thought Socks to himself.

"Hello are you there" Hester enquired. "Hello" "Yes yes I am here" Socks replied. "I know that this is probably quite a strange call for you to receive, but I'll get to the point", please do thought Socks to himself. "I am at Strathclyde Uni doing a degree in Psychology & am doing a paper on the sex industry", as you do thought Socks to himself. "Well I am just trying to work out where to start & then I remembered your gig in Edinburgh & remembered about the business card" there was a pause "go on" Socks said. "Ok, I was wondering if you would mind awfully if you would meet me, I know it is very cheeky of me to phone you out of the blue like this & you have every right to tell me where to go" Socks was thinking to himself how incredibly polite this girl was, there was something in her voice that he quite liked. "don't worry about it" replied Socks to something that was more of a statement than a question. "What is it that you want to know". "well, how you became a stripper, what your lifestyle is like, what you really think of woman, has doing this job changed your perception of woman, do you manage to shut off after doing gigs or do you still strut about as if you are doing a gig when you are back in normal day activities", usual stuff thought Socks to himself. The sort of questions girls ask you after you have finished your gig. "Yip, no problem, I'll meet you if you want, how about tomorrow night", "Oh thank you so very very much" replied Hester, "that is so awfully decent of you". "No worries, how about I meet you in Bar Kandi in hope st at say 8pm", "that will be fine" replied Hester. "I'll remember what you look like so I'll find you, thank you oh so very much once again". "See you tomorrow night" said Socks, "goodbye Socrates" replied Hester.

Socks went for a piss, ring ring , ring ring, his land line went. Damn, he tried to nip it half way through the streamie. "I'm coming" he shouted at the phone as a wet patch appeared on his blue bhs boxer shorts. It was Hero, "awright ma son" asked Hero, "awright me old cocker spaniel" replied Socks. "How was sunny Aberdeen", "not very sunny, it was a c**t of a drive, loads of hgvs & caravans, I left myself short of time & had to horse it, done it in two & a half though. "Any scandal" enquired Hero. "Nope, nothing, the poontang was good & pretty young, just a bunch of 18-20s acting up cause all their friends were there. It was bread & butter though, two fifteen minute spots, got the dosh & hit the road". "You couldn't get your hole in a barrel of fannies" laughed Hero. "Shut it you, anyways i've got your commission, give me a couple of hours & I'll fire over and see you", said Socks. "No worries brother, don't forget you owe me that commission for Saturday as well for that John gig" replied Hero, "Yeah man i've got it all here, see you soon"

Ok back to that streamie, Aaaaah full flow, ring ring, ring ring, "oh f**k right off" Socks shouted. This time he let it go on the answer machine. Aaah finished, shake shake. Any more than two shakes is a wank, Socks thought to himself, shake shake shake shake shake, as he walked into the back to the bar to get one for himself. Hester took a deep breath, why was she so nervous. She did not know what to wear so decided to play it safe & had opted for comfort over fashion. She was wearing a pair of Levi 501's, the first pair she had every bought & managed to fit into after loosing the weight over the last six months. She also had a Strathclyde Uni sweatshirt on & a pair of trainers. Socks returned from the bar & Hester started talking nine to the dozen (which she always done when she was nervous). She started talking about her course. Socks sat back and let her do the talking. He sized her up. She was small in height with a slight figure, pretty flat chested. Quite plain looking, but with lovely bright hazel brown eyes & very fair complexion. Nice short brown hair, kinda done in a old fashioned style. She had a kind aura about her. She kinda shined in a girl next door kinda way. Socks decided that he liked her straight away. She was extremely polite. He listened to what she had to stay & did not interrupt. Socks was a good listener, partly because he was reasonably polite himself in his own way & partly because he had been trained that way in various jobs. Going on many HR courses 'listening skills', 'time management skills', 'advanced boabey swinging skills'.

"So Socrates" said Hester, "tell me how you got into this whole stripping malarky". "Actually Hester, I think we should start with you, how does a nice clean cut girl like yourself end up doing a paper on the sex industry" replied Socks, "and another thing, please call me Socks, everybody calls me Socks". "Well Socks, what makes you think that I am a clean cut girl" replied Hester, "because I have been entertaining females for over ten years & I don't mean to sound big-headed or egotistic but these ten years have taught me a thing or two about woman". Hester backed down slightly & decided to tell Socks a story about a female that he would not hear every day.

Hester told Socks about her upbringing in Dunoon as a Vicars daughter. She told him how she had been frightened most of her life about 'real life'. How she envied all her friends because they seemed so full of life, so ready to unfold their arms to lifes experiences & not be scared, unlike Hester. She was always looking for excuses not to go to a pub or a nightclub, sometimes she even felt uncomfortable going shopping in Glasgow with her friends because she looked so dowdy, so plain. Men would always chat up her friends & she would be ignored, unless it was the really drunk guy who was too pissed to care who he was chatting up. She would even walk along the High St in Dunoon with her head down looking at the ground, she had no confidence. If somebody spoke to her she would jump out her skin. Jesus was her only true friend, she would talk to him all the time & he would comfort her. He would tell her that everything would be alright & that he loved her & that she was special & one day she would bloom into this beautiful flower, but the time had not arrived yet.

Socks listened without saying a word, he felt an incredible empathy for this girl.

"Socks, have you ever seen the Brian De Palma movie called Carrie" Hester asked. "Yes I am a huge movie fan & love De

Palma's work" replied Socks. "Well you know how Carrie's mum is fanatically religious & abuses Carrie", "Yes" replied Socks. "Well I cannot truly compare myself to Carrie as my parents are both wonderful people & have never raised a hand to me & barely even shouted at me as a kid, but there is still damage there, you know getting brought up in that kind of way, that strict Christianity". "Hold on here Hester, I hope you are not going to tell me that you are about to magically block the exits to the pub & put the place on fire with your mind & burn us all to death like in the Carrie movie" joked Socks. Hester laughed, it made the atmosphere a bit lighter, things were getting a bit on the heavy side for old Socky boy. "Yeah you had better not upset me then Socks, as I might just do that", "Oh noooo" laughed Socks. "Another analogy would be the movie Witness with Harrison Ford" said Hester, "have you seen that". "Yeah only about ten times, it's a classic" replied Socks, "I love that scene where Kelly McGillis gets her boobs out for a wash in the tub & old Harrison's is just standing there having a good swatch at them, trying to decide whether it is really worth it trying to get a shot on the swings with this bird or whether if barn burns on the knees might be a bit too painful seeing as they don't have any carpets or beds as they all sleep in hammocks. I mean have you ever tried having a shag in a hammock, it's not easy I'll tell you" joked Socks. "Had many hammock shags have you" asked Hester, "one or two" laughed Socks. "Anyways, we seem to be drifting of the point here" said Hester, "eh yeah what is the point exactly" retorted Socks. "I'm getting to that, the analogy I am trying to make is that the Amish lead a certain type of life, a very alternative life to normal every day society. When confronted with Harrison Ford & the baddies in the movie trying to kill him & the wee Amish boy, then they don't know how to behave, their immediate reaction is too cower away, to run away. "Fight or flight" intervened Socks. "Exactly" replied Hester. "Well that is how I feel when coming into the big cities, my upbringing has been so staid, rural & yes pretty strict, that I am like a shrinking violet, every time I was faced with something alien to me". "I here what you are saying" replied Socks, "but you could make another analogy for other people from their type of background", "how do you mean" replied Hester. She was pleasantly suprised with Socks, She had not really known what to expect, probably the stereotype male stripper, you know all tan & muscle & no brains, but he seemed different, reasonably intelligent & witty. Yes he definitely interested her. "Well" said

Socks. "Take the movie Wall St for instance, you could say that was a rich kids archetypical movie. Successful business man father sends his kids through private schools, gets the best education money can buy, no expense spared. Holidays four times a year in Florida Keys, he's got a place over there, got a car & a boat. The thing is he works so hard that he only ever really see's his kids at the weekend & sometimes not even then. So the kid grows up not really knowing his father. Then he goes to University, but it is the best in the land. Then he leaves and goes to work for some blue chip company. "Is this your life your talking about Socks" said Hester, "Hahahaha" laughed Socks, "no I am the exact opposite of that, but i've known these guys and from my experience they are very one dimensional characters, no real understanding of 'real life' or no real sense of humour, yeah they are generally hard work to be around" said Socks. "Ok I understand where you are coming from" explained Hester, "but let me tell you some more, do you want another drink".

Hester continued to explain about her past. How she had met her husband to be Alastair in the bible class meetings. How he was a wonderful man & was a lawyer. He was a partner at a practice in Glasgow & was a good bit older than her. His mother had lived in Dunoon and would frequently visit her at weekends, this is when he joined the bible study class.They had married three years ago, she reminded Socks of the gig in Edinburgh & how drunk she had been & totally out of character & had thrown up outside the gig. Socks laughed, but couldn't remember her. She explained how she had gotten pregnant & that was when things went wrong. She was convinced that Alastair was having an affair only six months after they had tied the knot. She found out the he was sleeping with his secretary. She decided to end the marriage. He tried to talk her out of it but she did not want to be with a man who would take his vows so lightly & run into the arms of another woman when she had his baby inside him. So she had a son called Connor & he was nearly two. He was the light of her life. Years ago she had done a HNC in Social Sciences and had never really used it to get a job in the 'real world'. She decided to expand on that qualification & was accepted at Strathclyde for the Physcology Degree. She started three months ago & was sharing a flat in Queen Margaret drive in the West End of Glasgow with five other students. Her parents were watching Connor & she would go home every Wednesday as there was no classes & every weekend, so she got to spend three fulls days with him. She missed him loads when she wasn't there but told herself that she was doing this for him.

Socks listened & thought that Hester was a very brave woman.

The thing was that although she had gone through all these life changes, her confidence was still low. No surprise considering what Alastair had put her through. So there was the chance of doing this paper on the sex Industry as a research project into looking at the men and women who work in that industry & the choices that they have made. So she wasn't just wanting to talk to strippers, she would interview prostitutes, male & female escorts, people who work in porn shops, maybe even people who take part in porn movies. She thought that this life experience would bring her more out of her shell & open up her mind.

"Bring you out of your shell, open up your mind" said Socks, "that's an understatement if I have every heard one". "what do you mean" asked Hester. "Well Hester you might find that you will get your mind opened wider than you expected, there are a lot of dodgy characters involved in this business & it is million miles away from Vicars tea party in Dunoon". "Oh could you possibly be more patronising" retorted Hester, "I am not a little girl anymore you know, you think you are so worldly wise don't you" she was getting angry now. She was more than aware that she was a Vicars daughter from Dunoon & didn't require to be reminded of the fact. "actually no, I don't think that, if I was so worldly wise I wouldn't be a bleeding stripper" replied Socks. "Just don't go into this with your eyes closed is all that I am saying & I am not trying to patronise you, I think that you are a very brave woman for what's its worth". Hester blushed, she was not used to getting many compliments & that one was not expected. "Anyway" said Hester, "enough about me, what about you, how did you get involved in this mental business. Socks went on to explain how he had been into working out & bodybuilding from sixteen years old. By the age of nineteen he was totally hooked. His life evolved around it. He would train four times a week, Tuesday, Thursday & both Saturday & Sunday. He would train so hard it was as if his life depended upon it. Every workout was a mission. He loved the way the training made him feel & look. He loved the way he felt after a workout, I don't just mean pumped up, but knackered in a chilled out at peace with the world kind off way. His life was very regimented, he worked loads of 9-5 jobs. He liked that form of working as it gave him a good routine to split his meals into five smaller meals a day rather than three larger ones. He could also get plenty of rest this way also. He wasn't much of a party animal back then, although he was making up for it now, usually either just a Friday or Saturday night, a pub then usually a cheesy nightclub. He was crap at chatting up girls, both him and his best mate back then were both pretty shy at approaching girls. (Hester thought that this was very amusing). Then one night after returning home from another gruelling workout, his father informed him that there had been an advert in the Evening Times, where some guy was looking for Scottish versions of the Chippendales. Well the rest as you know is history. Socks told Hester about meeting Mark & about the Pizza Hut sessions on a Saturday & Sunday, about his inauguration into the stripping game & about the other guys in the Highlanders, how they had been the best bunch of guys he had ever met in his life & how they would forever be his friends. Over the years some of them would lose contact, but the memories of what they had seen & done together would stay with them forever.

Hester, when I am an old fart sitting with the rest of the coffin dodgers in some home surrounded by Carers wiping porridge of my chin & shit of my arse, the memories of what I have done with the Highlanders will sustain me until my pish ridden corpse is pushing up the daises. Hester laughed out loud ! "You are mental Socrates", "takes one to know one Ms McCready" retorted Socks.

"Blow my whistle bitch, blow my whistle bitch", Sock's mobile ring-tone interrupted the laughter. "Deekster Boy, what's happening" Socks yelled into the mini-radiation spreading device. Socks hanged up, "Hester I am really sorry but I have to bolt, I have been offered a last minute gig in a house in Livingston, some guy has let them down & I have been called in to salvage it", "Owww" replied Hester. "I am not working during the day at the moment & need all the gigs I can get", "How about some other time" asked Hester. "No problem, listen will you let me take you for a meal & I promise that I will turn my phone off" asked Socks confidently. Hester blushed, she was not expecting that. "Of course I'll totally understand if you would rather not be seen twice with the same deviant male stripper", "shut up" laughed Hester still embarrassed. "Socks I would love to have a meal with you, thanks so much for asking" (god this girl is sooooo polite thought Socks to himself, but I definitely like her). "No worries, I've got too shoot, I'll phone you later" He shaked her hand goodbye & gave her a peck on the cheek. Hester stared after him as he hurried out of the pub. He was really nice, she thought to herself. I don't believe he asked me for a meal. Was it a date ? or was it just another business meeting ? what would she wear ? God she didn't have anything decent to wear ! This called for drastic measures, new shoes, shiny ones with diamontes, but not too shiny & not too many diamontes. Plus a new handbag, you can't buy new shoes & not buy a new handbag, what sort of handbag though ? one with a strap or one with a clasp ? black or brown ? noooo, she knew "RED", nooo he might think that she was too brazen if she turned up with a red handbag. Jesus, oooh sorry Jesus, God. oooh sorry God ! What about a dress ? Or would she better with a trouser suit, no, too formal. How about a skirt suit then, yes she had a nice cream coloured skirt suit, she would wear it with silky see through white blouse with that expensive £25 bra out of Debenhams. How about jewellery, some nice delicate Rennie Macintosh would do the trick, earrings & necklace & just one ring on her right hand. What about makeup ?

"Oh for Christ sake, he will buy you a meal then try and get into your knickers, he's a bloody stripper. he will just want a shag Hester & then you'll never see hide or hair of him again" said Marsie. "Marsie don't say Christ like that, you know I don't like it" replied Hester. Marsie was also doing the same degree as Hester & they had become good friends. "Anyway" said Hester speaking into the phone, "You can't just judge people like that, he seems like a really nice guy", "aye right, all I am saying is just don't trust him, he's probably got a silver tongue from all these years of stripping. Just make sure he wears a condom" "MARSIE", shouted Hester, "I am not going to have sex with him, he'll probably not even call again".

"Where do you come from where do you go, cotton eye Joe" Hester's mobile ring-tone screeched out. "Marsie, Marsie, it's him on my mobile, I'll call you straight back". "Hello" said Hester, "Hester, Hi it's Socks here" "Hi Socks" said Hester trying to keep the excitement from her voice, "listen Hester I am still at the gig, I have done my first spot & have to go back on again in two minutes, I just wanted to apologise on running out on you like that. I would really like to take you for a meal to make up for it & to discuss your paper further", "you don't have to apologise Socks, no problem" replied Hester.

"Listen" said Socks, "I know a really nice Chinese restaurant in Balloch, are you free on Thursday night this week", "Yes that sounds lovely" replied Hester. "Ok cool, I'll text you on Thursday afternoon & we'll make arrangements", "Ok see you Thursday Socks" said Hester, "see you Thursday" said Socks & hung up. Marsie's phone rang, "Hi Hester", "Marsie, I need you to come shopping with me","Blow my whistle bitch, blow my whistle bitch", "Hero" said Socks answering his phone. "Are you home yet son" asked Hero, "Nope just on the road home bro" replied Socks. "How was it" asked Hero, "bread & butter, fifteen in the living room, that boy from Edinburgh let them down. Blade or something like that". "Glasgow boy to the rescue then" retorted Hero. "Yeah something like that man", "whenever they came out with their weegie comments, I just reminded them who had pulled the cat out of the bag for them" said Socks. "Hero, you know how I told you about the Vicars daughter", "Yeah man, what about her", "well I met her tonight before doing this gig", "so I take it she had a Laurie Ashley dress on down to her toes & fastened up to her neck, carrying a bible & trying to convert you to Christ" laughed Hero. "No man, she was really nice, really polite & I mean really polite, I don't think that I have ever met somebody quite like her", "you sound smitten bro, so when you seeing her again". "Well laughed Socks, Thursday night actually, I'm taking her for a Chinese meal". "Then back to yours for a shot on the swings eh" laughed Hero. "Not at all, I wouldn't dream of it", laughed Socks. "Anyway I've got a feeling that she is not that type of a girl" said Socks. "What you mean, somebody that's got taste" joked Hero, "very funny" laughed Socks.

"So Hero me old cocker spaniel", "Yes old Socky boy, how can I be off assistance", "well, what do you think I should wear", "Hmmm, I know how about your U2 boots & do you still have that barber jacket", cackled Hero. "F**k off you" snorted Socks.

"Eh so Hero, seriously, what do you think I should wear............"

Ten

"Read all about it, read all about it, Scotland's premier male dance troupe, The Highlanders dominate the Scottish Media for three years from 1991 to 1994. They appear on terrestrial TV channel STV on Scottish Women & Scottish Men, they appear on cable TV. They are covered in popular tabloids, the Daily Record, Evening Times, The Sun, The News of the World, The Sunday Mail, they even break down the barriers of the huffy broadsheets, yes yes it's true, they appear in the Glasgow Herald & the Scotsman. The local rags are not to be left out either with the Clydebank Post even getting in on the action, read all about it, read all about it"......

The Sun photographer was fussing about with his volopter plopter five billion trillion pixel camera. He removed his snotty hanky from his jacket lapel pocket, gave it a gay wave in the air, fifty hardened snott residues plastered everybody and anybody in the close proximity of the studio, like a nail bomb in a shopping mall in the Middle East. Mark was on the phone giving it his usual "buy buy, sell sell". The strippers were all standing in their boxers shorts, well Hero had his usual bombers (aka briefs) on, as ! "Well, he liked everything to be compactly held in place" (weidro). Melanie the Coordinator came rushing into the studio. "I've got them, i've got them". She held up five copies of Kay Adams face on a 6" x 5" print. The photographer wiped his double glazing lens with his less snotty hanky. "Right lads, if you can just mosey on over here please". So the lads did a bit of moseying, aligned themselves against the studio photoshoot backdrop. They looked like they were in a Police line-up. The porn actress would come in wearing a nurses uniform with white stockings and white high heel shoes (please !), she would be escorted by a female police officer & would be sobbing. The guys would be asked to drop their pants & the porn actress would point at Levi and say "yes Officer he's the one with the massive cock, he he he tried to choke me with it during the blow job scene". Ahem ! "right lads" said the photographer, "if you can just drop your pants & hold Kay Adams in front of your cocks", "sorry", replied Dog, "I'm not that sort of boy", "ooh er Matron" replied Brutus", "don't you mean in front of our big cocks" snorted Hero. The photographer sighed, the coordinator sniggered. "Just get on with it you lot" shouted Mark, "yes oh wise one" replied Socks.

The Guys had appeared on Scottish Women the previous week & the Sun wanted in on the action while it was hot. So there was the guys on page 3 of the Sun that Friday. All the builders & labourers & sparks & joiners were in for a shock that day. There they were with their pies & Forfar bridies & cans of Irn Bru ready for their early morning perv when low & behold five bears with a picture of Kay Adams over their bell-ends springs out at them.

Socks looks at the clippings fifteen years later & smiles to himself. There was Brutus looking like a cardboard cut-out. Looking like the dude out of the John Smiths advert. There was Hero who looked like he had a crick in his neck & was about to fall over (weebles wobble but they don't fall down), Dog didn't look much better, he looked like somebody you had just given bad news to, but they weren't really listening, so they are still smiling that stupid false kinda smile haha. That photographer must have hated us.

He came across the one of the Scotsman, that was his favourite, it was Pat Kanes wife out of Hue & Cry who was the reporter. She had done a very witty write up on the guys. He liked the line about the average punter at the gig in the Gorbals where she had covered the story "She had forearms like Maw Broon" har har brilliant.

Then there was the one of Dog holding the calculator in front of his mush, he looked as if somebody had shoved a banana up his bacy & was enjoying it. It was the old brawn & brain angle. He was supposed to have an IQ of 135 although I have a feeling that there should be a decimal point in there somewhere.

Saying that though there was some cracking professional shots. We had done a few photography sessions in Studio Scotland in Trongate in Glasgow and there was a few favourites that the press liked to use. Yip some right mean & moody shots. You know the type, square jaw, hair immaculate, that v-tapered, ripped, lean, vascular, bright eyed, young, dumb & full of cum ! People that met us on our travels used to always ask us "Guys what kinda diet are you on ? do you take steroids ? do you take supplements & if so what ones" ? Well the truth of the matter was that yes we did eat reasonably well, chicken, fish, pasta, rice, fruit & veg, BUT, and that is a very big BUTT, we also ate a lot of shite. Ask the Manager of the China Sea Chinese restaurant in Gordon St in Glasgow. We were there every week for nearly three years. We must have been his best customers. If we knew that we were running late from a gig, we used to phone up & Michael the Manager with the worst toupee you've seen in your life would let us order our main courses over the phone & they would be ready when we arrived. We would eat Mcdonalds, KFCs', Burger Kings.We would eat anything. No we wouldn't take steroids & we all loved it when people thought we did. We did take supplements, Creatine, a lean mass stimulator that would flood your muscles with water & make you appear bigger. We would take inosine which would make you train like Arnie. If we were getting a bit flat looking then we would take HMB Hydroxide methol butyrate, this would act as a catalyst fat burner & would give you that "ripped" look. Basically though we trained like demons possessed & and the gigs were like workouts themselves, we would sometimes dance for thirty minutes during the finale & would come off-stage sweating like rapists during a prison riot. We were also mad clubbers. We would do a two hour gig then horse it back to Glasgow to go to the Tunnel nightclub or the Arches, we would get in for the two o'clock curfew & dance our pants of for the last hour and a half. That is why we were in good shape. Healthy living, loads of rest and sleep, bollox. We lived the opposite way a bodybuilder was suppose to live. Getting by on a couple of hours sleep a night was common place, we were always playing sleep catch up. Most of the guys held down full time jobs. In the early years it was common place to do three or four gigs a week. You were also trying to train three or four times a week as well as socialising & possibly holding down a relationship. We were all high on life & we needed a healthy dose of it to maintain our addiction ! We walked through life buzzed up, we would do gigs & get buzzed up, we would train like our life's depended upon it & get buzzed up, we would shag our girlfriends & get buzzed up, then the day jobs would drag us down. Being a work slave 9-5 or 12-8 or whenever we worked was the reality check, this was the daily dose of cold turkey to bring us crashing back down to earth.

"Working for the Man
it didn't work for Cool Hand Luke
it didn't work for the Rebel without a cause
because
brain numbing commute doesn't compute
the computer
sitting astride the personal work station
standing at the train station
it blinks with its cursor in your face
save me from this dreaded place

plaice for tea again, fish on the menu
I dream of better days
Dazed and confused
I tie the tie
tie me down
Don't make me wear the working man's crown
frown once, frown twice
take me to a place away from here
here, it's Sunday night
cold and clammy, my hands are
whats wrong with me ??
it's not the job you see !!
it's not doing what is meant
the purpose
everybody has one
find it
search high and low
find the light
but there is no tunnel
steam train racing down the track
white horses, men astride
Butch Cassidy & Sundance side by side
working for the man
it's not their game plan....."

Kay Adams opened up the Sun to page 3. She couldn't believe that she had bought this rag. When her agent phoned and told her that her face was splattered over the Highlanders boabeys she had laughed out loud. They had been very entertaining on her show. The ratings had been very good that night. What was it that guy Hercules or Socrates or something had said "we get all types of women going to our show, extroverted, introverted, but at the end of the night, they all go wild" haha. Yes she had enjoyed that show immensely. Here they were now, the cheeky monkeys with my face hiding their crotch. She was quite pleased, it was a half decent photo, thank God she had got it done the previous week. She nibbled on her carrot cake & took a sip of her coffee. They were supposed to do a routine (keeping the clothes on) on the show but there had been some sort of technical problem. The sound guy probably couldn't get the baby oil stains of their show cd. She chuckled to herself. There was some charity doe coming up that she could maybe get the guys to do, once again keeping their clothes on. She didn't want to get into hot water with her producers.

"Dog, has the Markster phoned you about the meet tomorrow night" enquired Hero."Not yet man, what's up" replied Dog. "He's all excited about something, something to do with Harry Margolis & a trip to China", "whit a tour do you mean" asked Dog. "yeah man, something like that" replied Hero.

Ring ring, ring ring, "hello" answered Levi, "Levi me old cocker spaniel" said Brutus, "whits happening man" enquired Levi. "Has Mark phoned you about this Japan thing", said Brutus, "I thought it was China" answered Levi, "same difference man" retorted Brutus. "well actually Brutus my good fellow, it is not the same thing, there is a large geographical differences & the cultural differences are huge also, not to mention the history & religious impact also", "shut it you" said Brutus, "Ok so you have heard, what do you make of it", "sounds pretty damn amazing if it is true, I can't imagine that they have had much in the way of male strippers in China", "nope neither do I" said Brutus, "they have had plenty of experience on the poontang angle though, what with I love you long time & hey GI you wannae fuckie fuckie, suckie suckie, twenty dolla, for twenty dolla I love you long time" drolled Brutus. "Well actually you ignoramus" replied Levi "I do believe you are referring to Vietnam & Cambodia, which both once again have massive Geographical & historical/cultural differences", "f**k you" retorted Brutus, "no I do believe you mean fuckie fuckie you" laughed Levi. They both laughed. "Hey Levi you watch too many inaccurate American war movies" said Brutus.

The Guys all met up at the Holiday Inn in Glasgow at the bar. Mark dipped his hands into his pockets & bought the first round. He then got all their attention, sucked in his ever expanding waist & blew out his chest, cleared his throat. We all waited with baited breath. "Guys, how do you all fancy going to China for a months tour, then coming back, moving into the same house, a company six bedroom house and driving about in a company car each. Probably a BMW.

The Guys all looked at each other with their mouths hanging open. They then shut their mouths & turned back to face their smiling Manager.

Eleven

It was the 16th October 1994. Mark explained what was laid out in the last chapter. For three years the Highlanders had been in the spotlight. This is had not gone unnoticed from the powers that be. Harry Margolis had probably the biggest Entertainment agency in Glasgow. He had given the dance troupe a lot of work over these three years & watched them grow from strength to strength. A major Chinese Entertainment agent had been over to Scotland to do the tourist bit. He done the whole Edinburgh Castle thing. He came through to Glasgow & visited a few of the distilleries, he even went over to a couple of the Scottish Islands to visit the remote distilleries & whisky bonds. While he was over he bought some of the tabloids & saw an article on the Highlanders. He was sitting with his wife in the Hilton in Glasgow watching TV when Scottish Women came on & the Highlanders appeared. An idea formed in his head & he done a bit of digging & got Harry's contact number. He didn't phone it until a month later. He had contacted the Chippendales Management Company in the States & the price they tried to charge was extortionate. Then Men of Texas were also very expensive. He then set his sights on the UK & to London to the Dream Boys, they weren't too bad. Then he contacted Harry & the bargain basement Highlanders & the wheels got set in motion. After this enquiry Mark decided that he was going for world domination. Today Scotland, tomorrow China, we had already done Spain, so the rest of the world the day after tomorrow. He laid out his plan out of how he would market this incredible feat. It had to be said that back then in the good old days, we were pretty damn gullible, so as much as I would like to kid yourself & myself on that we scoffed at Mark's plans. We sucked them in like a sherbet dip. We sat wide eyed & bushy tailed and listened to the tale of high adventure that Peter Jackson's Lord of the Rings could only dream of getting close to. He was wanting to lease a Company house, he was thinking Bishopbriggs or Kirkintilloch which are reasonably affable areas of Glasgow. This would be the centre of operations & he would live there also & would double up as an office. We would each be getting a company car also on a lease deal. It would be a prestige car. We were excited, it was easy to understand why, we had been in the forefront for three years & were getting carried away with the media attention. You tell yourself, "why not me, why can't it be my turn". The answer of course is very apparent. It can be answered in one word "GREED". China didn't happen, the house didn't happen & the cars didn't happen. The thing was the house and the cars weren't ever really going to happen, but China should have. Greed stopped it due to a combination of Mark & Harry kicking the c**t out of it. Harry was trying to get Mark to take far less money than was fair, Mark counter-attacked that by giving a price that was totally unreasonable. Harry then added a shitload onto that price and went back to the Chinese dude, who probably just laughed and phoned the Dream Boys. To this day, I don't know if any strippers went over to China on that deal. I would like to think they did. At the start of the 21st century the East West relations were improving vastly, ten years earlier it would have probably been unthinkable to consider such a move. Saying that the East West relations might not have been so strong after sending the Highlanders. It might have set them back another hundred years.

So before Mark broke the bad news to us that it had gone all tits up, which took about a month. That month was gravy, we walked tall, our eyes met our fellow man in the street, we rose from the gutter, we had made it, we were successful, the American dream in Glasgow. Of course it is a well known Scottish tradition to take your fellow man down a peg or two when they are doing well. So we got our fare share of "ach, it won't happen, it's just a pipe dream" or "China, you've more chance of going tae Cardiff". Then of course the inevitable "I told you so", although from close family & friends you knew if was restrained, because for that short four weeks they shared your dream.

As I said though, for the four weeks, we lived the dream and we planned. "So Hero my old son, whit car are you going to get" enquired Socks, "well old Socky boy me tinks that moi will get a Ford Capri Brooklands 3.0L and do it up, reconditioned engine, new alloys, new recaro seats, sound system of death", "whit" laughed Dog, "Hero, you wont be able to get anything like that, it will be new or nearly new. It will be a pool of cars", "yeah man" said Levi, "according to the Markster, it will be a prestige car not a bleeding sport car, so your talking about an BMW, Merc, Saab or an Audi", "I'm going for a black beamer coupe 320" said Socks, "I've always had a thing for black bmw's", "Naw, you shouldn't get a Beemer or a Merc" said Hero. "Why not man" asked Socks looking baffled. "well there's a good reason why socks" replied Hero, "well is it a bloody secret or what" asked Socks laughing. "Well yeah actually it is kinda a secret actually & if I tell you guys you must promise never to repeat it to another living soul" said Hero with a serious tone and a kinda mystical wisdom, "well" replied Dave, "I promise never to say a word to anybody, apart from yer Ma when I am climbing of her at the weekend". They all fell about laughing, expect for Hero "what do you mean". He waited until the hilarity died done to a murmur & then got up and closed the door & beckoned the guys to gather round him. He started whispering "guys the insignia of the Mercedes car & the BMW ie the badge" he looked around him and back at the door to make sure that nobody was coming in. "well" said Socks. "The badge is the sign of Satin, of Lucifer, of the Devil", "WHAT" yelled Dog & Levi in unison. Hero continued, "the badge on the mercedes car is an inverted cross that Jesus was crucified on for our sins, think about the shape of it. It is an upside down cross. The BMW badge although not as obvious is also an inverted cross, think about the design and the way the badge is joined up in three sections, it is an upside down cross" Hero stopped and looked at the Guys. They were all staring around at each other. "He's right you know Guys" said Dog, "I never thought of it before, but it is an inverted cross". "Does that then mean" started Socks, "Yes" said Hero, "anybody that owns a Mercedes or BMW is an apostle of Lucifer", "but" said Levi, "no buts" said Hero "it's not got to be butter", "but" said Levi again, "to make you understand" said Hero, "these are not bad people that buy BMW's or Mercedes", "when they buy them they are good people or reasonably good people, but the Devil makes them evil, one day they are good mannered people going about they're daily business, the next they just turn into wankers......not thanking you on the motorway for letting them in, cutting you off every chance they get, flashing their lights at you in the fast lane to let them by", "hahahaha you bastard Hero" laughed Socks. "Man you had me totally taken in there" yelled Dog, "bastard" said Levi & Brutus in unison. "So Hero" said Socks, "what car are you going to get", "well, probably a BMW or Mercedes" laughed Hero. The Guys all fell about laughing again.

"I think I'll go for that new Audi A4, you know the one with the twin exhaust pipes" said Levi, "you shouldn't buy Audi" said Hero. "Shut up you" laughed Levi. "Nah good choice my man" said Hero "it's a nice brief". "What about you Dog" asked Socks, "No competition" replied Dog "Saab 900 turbo" that thing has got wings. "I'll go with Socks" injected Brutus, "I am quite fond of a

Black beemer as well", "you've got good taste man" said Socks, "anyway in a few years time Maxi Jazz from Faithless is going to write a song about cars & he is going to use the lyrics "drive that black bm home once again". I am going to like these lyrics & that is another reason I will be getting a beamer. "Eh ok man, whatever" said Dog. "What about you Dave" asked Dog, "I don't believe that you are included in this company car scheme are you mate", "piss right of you" laughed Dave. "Maybe Mark will get you a Lada or a Skoda or something Mate" said Socks. "Yer BMW is getting keyed in the first week ya fat bastard" retorted Dave. Hahaha ! "Dave it's ok mate you can go on my insurance for my Saab" laughed Dog, "I'll drive yer Saab up yer arse followed by Socks & Brutus's Beemers" scowled Dave. Hahaha !

"What about the house sketch Dave" said Socks, "Do you think Mark will let you sleep down the cellar or something", "F**k you Socks" said Dave. "Yeah there should be a spare cupboard in the kitchen, you and all yer belongings, yer decks, all yer choons & you can live in there" said Hero, "F**k you" as well Hero. "I'll tell you what ya bunch of widos" said Dave, "once you have all moved into yer shitty house & are tucked up nice and tight by daddy Mark, I'll burn yer c**t of a house to the ground" joked Dave. "Oooooh nasty nasty Dave" said Brutus, "Oh come on big smile Eddie" laughed Socks.

"Yo Hero" shouted Dog down the phone. "I take it you have just had Marky Mark on the blower" enquired Hero. "Yeah Man, China's not happening" said Dog. "Yeah the two greedy bastards made a c**t of it" said Hero. "I sometimes wish that we would just look after our own interests and this shit wouldn't happen" said Hero. "Yeah dude I know what you mean, an agent is meant to take 15% and a manager up to 30%. Which is 45% all in, whits the bets that they have taken 100% ie doubled the price of the whole deal the greedy thieving bastards" replied Dog.

"So what do we do now" enquired Dog, "I don't know about you Dog, but I off to see Dave" said Hero. "Dave, what can Dave do" replied Dog. "Nothing" answered Hero. "I need to borrow his Lada".

Twelve

The Islands Tour (Part 1)

Mary daughter of Marcus peered through her living room window. The rain was pelting down. It was the middle of October & the trees were shedding their leaves. She had a big oak in her front garden. It used to frighten her as a child. It stood in the dark when she was going to bed like a midnight dinosaur, poised, ominous & threatening with its outstretched arms, waiting to snatch the life out of her as she sleeped. She shuddered with the memory of it. Then she frowned, what a shit day for the strippers to be arriving.

Her boyfriend Adam son of Allan had booked the Highlanders for a one night only gig on the Isle of Mull where they lived. Mull was one of the Scottish western Isle's & one of the favourite for tourists. It had loads of history. Great trails for hiring a mountain bike or off-road 4 x 4. Amazing scenery, but also a great Town/Village with Tudor style houses & buildings, a lovely scenic marina and even some smashing pubs & a trendy club, where the Highlanders were due to play.

Adam was a promoter & DJ for the club. He had brought over loads of DJs & even some bands. Female strippers as well, the UK Calendar Girls (they were gorgeous), but this was the first time that he had booked male strippers. Adam was worried. He hadn't sold very many tickets & was dreading that it was going to be a flop. Saying that though Mull was like that, they had a reputation of turning up on the night last minute. It was a typical Scottish Island, the population consisted of pure blood Mull, born & bred there, non-pure blood Mull i.e. people from the large towns & cities who had come to live on Mull & raise families. The parents that came over were non-pure blood Mull, but because their children were born there, then they were pure blood. Then there was the people who came over to work there for the season, a combination of students from Glasgow & Edinburgh, even some from the mainland via Campbletown & Fort William. Then the foreign workers, usually working for buttons in the Hotel game, there was loads of them from Poland, Germany, Sweden, Denmark, Holland & Belgium. Usually if there was any cheap labour farming work or cherry/grape picking then you would find them doing that also. Finally there was the tourists, what it was all about, they kept the Island alive, during season they would flock from all over the world & Mull would thrive, but it was now October & everybody was battoning down the hatches for winter. Adam son of Allan scratched his chin and wondered why the hell he didn't try and bring them over during the summer months. What was he thinking about, they had cost a shit load of money & now it looked like he might be making a loss, a big loss.

Dog son of a gun wiped the window at his seat in the restaurant on the ferry, it was all condensate. All he could see was pelting rain, stormy seas & the horizon going up and down. His stomach leaped, aaah ! don't look out again he thought to himself, that just makes it worse. It was a particularly stormy day on the North Sea. There was gale force winds & a shit load of rain. The captain had his work cut out for him that day. They had considered cancelling this sailing but the weather report had said that the wind was to clear. How can these guys get it wrong all the time & still keep their jobs ?? A Car salesman doesn't sell a car in three months, Hey it's ok brother don't worry say the boss, here's a shit load of cash anyway, why ? well, because I like you, your alright & what's more you've been trying really hard & it's not your fault that you haven't even sold a Punto, so take all this cash & go have a great time. Right ! wrong ! life isn't like that, so how come these weather dudes keep getting it wrong. Me thinks we'll apply for a job as a weather man. "Hi Honey I'm home", "Hi sweetheart how was work today dear" ? "great honey, I made a rip roaring c**t of it again & my boss gave me a raise".

"Dog, what are you smiling about man" enquired Brutus, "weather men" replied Dog. "Eh" asked Brutus, "never mind, how much longer do we have in this tin can, I'm feeling sqweezy" replied Dog. "About another two hours mucker" said Hero. "Hey" said Socks, "have you counted the number of people on this boat wearing Shetland wool jumpers", "funnily enough, naw" said Dave. "Well I have and there are twelve people in this restaurant alone sporting them, and three are birds", "that is extremely interesting Socks" said Levi, "thank you so much for feeling the need to share that with us". "think about it" replied Socks, "if there is twelve people in this part of the ship alone wearing Shetland wool jumpers, how many will there be in the entire ship", "I dred to think" replied Hero. "anyway" said Dog, "how do you know that they are wearing Shetland wool & not say Orkney wool or something", "Oh yeah" replied Socks, "you normally hear of Orkney wool jumpers don't you, I think I'll just fire doon the shops & treat myself to a new Orkney wool jumper", the guys all laughed. "He's got a point Dog" said Hero. "Right" Socks, "operation Shetland under starting orders, I'm away to count the number of people wearing them on this boat, I'll return at 03 hundred hours, synchronize your watches", "whatever" shouted Hero as Socks headed for the port side.

Mary daughter of Marcus was getting ready, Adam son of Allan was picking her up in ten minutes. She opted for a pair of jeans (501's), a t-shirt, a pair of black boots, a Shetland wool jumper and a tea-cosy for a hat. Adam pulled up outside in his Subaru WRX & gave a honk, HONK ! They headed onto the west coast road and started the thirty minute drive to the ferry terminal. They headed away from the busy centre of the island and started to pass green fields with abandoned tractors & combines. They passed small cottages with smoke whisping out the chimneys, masses of trees with their leaves lying at their feet. The road twisted & turned. The oversized exhaust on the WRX spat out carbon monoxide fumes & roared onwards. There was plenty on Sunday drivers out on this wet Friday afternoon, Adam cursed them. There was your usual grannies in their Hyundai Getz (you knowhere fast) out for a wee afternoon drive, wearing their scone hats & scone shoes, caravans with families on vacation (but no Chevy Chase in sight), a few hgv's & your usual white van man (there everywhere, they are not just a common denominator of towns but a global disease). He horsed it past them all, leaving the bitter taste of his Scube fumes in their mouths. "There's the ferry" remarked Mary, "it's on time". "I wonder what they will be like", "probably totally up themselves, with perfect hair, skin & a six pack" retorted Adam.

"Did you remember the six-pack Dog" asked Levi, "yeah man, it's in the boot, I just got tennents, it'll do for the room while we get freshened up & changed". "forty-three" shouted Socks coming back to join the guys. "what" asked Dave. "Forty-three Shetland wool jumpers", "Oh shut up you" laughed Hero, "No, I'm telling you twenty-five guys, fifteen chicks, two kids & a dog" said Socks, "f**k off you" laughed Dave, "what you mean a dog" said Brutus, "eh doh ! a dog you know four legs, a canine, mans best friend and all that shite" retorted Socks. "It had one of these doggy coat things, but was made out of wool", "that's crazy" said Dave, "it's just going to get soaked in this weather", "yeah man phone the RSPCA, i'd like to report a wet dog". "Guys we've arrived and it's brightening up". Sorry weather man thought Dog to himself.

"Nice to meet you Adam" Said Hero, "I'm Hero, it's me you've been talking to on the phone", "Oh yes right" said Adam, "nice to meet you Hero, this is my girlfriend Mary", Mary waved a hi at the Guys, "This is Dog, Brutus, Levi, Socks & Dave" said Hero. "I'm the only one with a proper name" said Dave. They all laughed, that broke the ice. "How was your crossing guys" asked Mary, "choppy" replied Dog whose colour was just beginning to return. "I counted forty-three Shetland wool jumpers" said Socks. "sorry" said Mary, "but yours makes forty-four" said Socks. "Don't worry about him" said Hero frowning at Socks "he's the village idiot". "Oh we already have one of them" said Adam, "really" laughed Levi, "yes my brother Sammy", everybody laughed again. "Right guys if you'll just follow me we'll go to the club first, I need to set up some stuff, then I'll take you to the B & B". "No worries, lead on Mcduff" said Socks.

"Going to shut up about these stupid jumpers" said Hero to Socks once they were in the car. "they might think your patronizing them", "no worse than you man, you just called them stupid jumpers, they might not like that" laughed Socks. "Mary is a bit of alright eh" commented Brutus, "aye man she would get it" said Levi. "Yeah it's the Shetland wool jumper that done it for me" laughed Socks again. "Do you think they wear woolly knickers over here" said Dave, "aye man there called Damart" said Hero. "Hey Dave, know how you like these short skirts" said Hero, "yeah" said Dave, "well I don't think that you will see many over here, it's bloody freezin".

"So what do you think of them" Adam asked Mary. "Well they are nothing like the Chippendales" laughed Mary. "I like them though in a kinda cheeky, harder looking way", "yeah they seem like right characters" said Adam, "i'll tell you this though for nothing, I'm not leaving you alone with them for one minute, I wouldn't trust them as far as I could throw them, which isn't very far".

They pulled up at the club which was down at the harbour beside the marina. It was busy, there was a pub adjoined to the club, the pub was on the lower level & the club was upstairs. Everybody's heads turned as Mary, Adam & the five strangers, four of which you wouldn't want to meet on a dark night headed for the stairs. The guys were used to it, they just smiled at the girls & ignored the guys. It was the most unusual club they had ever seen. On one side was the dj booth on a kinda raised stage which would also double up for bands. Also a few tables besides it with chairs. On the other side was a tiered area with wooden seats on raised levels which can only be described as the sort of thing that you would see in a stadium or a school gym or at a swimming pool. There was about six different levels of these wooden seat/benches & there was kinda church pue in front of each bench for your drinks to go on. I don't know who designed that & worse still the club owner who agreed but they must all need their heads looked at. Saying that it might not have always been a club. Maybe it had been a school gym & they shipped it into the club. In the middle of course was the dancefloor, quite narrow but long.

Adam was setting up the decks, a pair of Technics, 1210's mark 1's, the silver ones. Industry standard, which any self respecting club had in their DJ booth. Also a large chunky Vestax mixer, quite an old one by the looks of it, but they were well made & would last for many years. Dave was busying himself around Adam. Socks was also paying a close interest. Socks quite fancied himself as a bit of a bedroom jock & had bought himself a pair of crappy belt drive el cheepo decks & an even crappier el cheepo mixer " Dave ask Adam If I can get a shot of the decks" said Socks. "ask him yourself ya fanny" replied Dave, "no, you" said Socks, "f**k off and ask him yourself ya wank, what are you all shy all of a sudden", "yes I am all shy all of a sudden", "so will you ask him", "no" said Dave.

"Adam my main man" said Socks, "what's up" replied Adam. "Well it's like this, I'm a bit of a bedroom DJ & was wondering if I could get a shot on the decks". "Yeah man no problem, what sort of stuff are you into" replied Adam. "Mainly trance, but not that cheesy female vocal shite, more of the deeper instrumental stuff", "nice one, I'm more into my funky house" said Adam. Socks busied himself picking out a couple of slices of vinyl & then setting them up for mix. "Hey Adam, where's the headphone mix cue switch" shouted Socks. "Sorry" replied Adam. "You know the cue switch/button thingy, where you can set up the mix in your cans before sending the mix out live", "Oh er that mixer hasn't got that, I've had a few guest DJ's over who have asked me that before". "Shite mixer" whispered Socks to Dave. "A bad workman blames the tools" replied Dave. "Your a f***ing tool ya nob" laughed Socks.

"Right guys I'll take you to the B & B" said Adam. "It's very homely" said Mary, "you'll like it". "As long as there is a bed I don't care" replied Hero. They settled thereselves into the B & B, it was very homely. The rooms had pictures of Victorian characters on the wall. They were wearing these silly looking wigs & had the frilly shirts on with the even frillier cuffs sticking out from the bottom of the jacket sleeves. "Hey Dog ,what's the picture of your dad doing on the wall" shouted Levi. "Shut it you" replied Dog, "It looks more like your maw than my dad". Brutus walked into the room, "who fancies going for a sorte down by the marina". "Sounds like a plan my man" replied Hero. "What a bloody view" said Socks. The guys were leaning on a wall down at the promenade" The weather had cleared up & the although it wasn't exactly sunny, it was dry, clear & cold. The vast expanse of the sea stretched out before them like a straight empty motorway, but without lines & without fields on either side. In fact it was nothing like a motorway. In the distance, the distant distance (is that a phrase ?) they could make out the silhouette of a cargo ship, probably carrying bananas or iron ore or something. There were also a couple of sailing boats bobbing up and down. "Isn't the sea amazing" asked Socks. "Hows that then Socks" replied Dog. "Well it's kind of mysterious & romantic in a dark & melancholy kind of way" retorted Socks. "Eh, what do you mean man" said Dog. "Ach your a heathen Dog, you either feel it or you don't" scowled Socks", "that's it, that's what I'm trying to say ! It's a feeling, the sea is a feeling, when you look at the sea, it makes you feel a certain way. It's hard to explain, but I suppose it goes back to childhood where your folks took you to Dunoon or Rothesay for the day & you travelled on the Caledonian Macbrayne ferries. As a kid you loved it, it was like an adventure". "Is that right" said Hero. "well it wasn't like that for me, I associate it with Dave the dude in the advert with the guy out swimming & goes out too far & then gets tired & is waving madly for help & then there's the old dude & his missus on the beach going, hey that guy is waving at us dear, so they wave back & then Dave is the dude who is telling you to be careful when your down the beach, and watch the tides etc" Hahaha, the guys all laughed. "Well it's well seeing that it's not our Dave" said Levi. "He would just let the man drown", "shut it you" retorted Dave scowling.

At 8pm the guys arrived at the club. The bar downstairs was getting busy & a band was setting up to entertain what was going to be a mainly male audience for the first part of the night as the chicks would be getting their rocks off upstairs with the lads. Adam was on the decks at 8.30 and was playing some upfront mainstream funky grooves to the so far rather quiet club. At 9 bells there was about thirty birds in & they looked hungry for boabey. The guys came onstage at 9.30 & there was another half dozen or so that had arrived. "Bloody all the way to Mull for thirty-six birds, smashing" commented Dave as he came into the dressing room/toilet to check if Hero was ready. "Tell us about it mate" replied Dog, "feel sorry for Adam though, he must be well embarrassed". "Embarrassed f**k all, he'll be worrying about the money he has got to pay us" frowned Brutus. "F**k it guys, we all know that it's about the jolly doing these tours, let's just make the best of it eh" said Socks. "Always the optimist dude" said Levi. So the guys gave it 110% and the girls seemed to enjoy themselves. Even the bird in the white lycra skimpy dress that launched herself at Brutus when he done the full monty. Poor guy shat himself. The Highlanders packed up their bags & headed downstairs to the main bar where the band was in full swing. "What you having to drink guys" said Adam, "and once again, I'm really sorry for the crappy turnout, I just don't understand this place at times". "Don't worry about it dude" replied Hero, "shit happens as the t-shirt says, get us five pints of bud & we'll call it quits", "no worries" laughed Adam. "Hey Socks, I thought you wanted a shot on the decks", "No it's ok man, can't be bothered" replied Socks. He turned to Dave "shite mixer".

The Girl with the white lycra dress approached the guys. "Hi Strippers, my names Mary, please to meet you all, I loved your show", "thanks very much Mary, that's very kind of you to say so" replied Socks, but she wasn't interested in Socks. She had already made her mind up who she was after & Brutus was it. She was in her mid-forties with long curly black hair, big brown eyes & even bigger lips with far too much make-up on. She had that kinda green eye shadow on, which actually made her look even older. Her breasts were hanging out of her low cut dress & she was bending over in front of Brutus's face to make sure he got a good eyefull. "What's your name handsome" Mary asked Brutus. "Eh my names Hero" said Brutus. Hero spat out his mouthful of Bud laughing. "Hoi you" he shouted at Brutus. "Well Hero, why don't you take a walk with me & I'll show you my lovely village". "Ok" said Brutus, "why not". He winked at the guys, Mary took his hand & they headed for the door. Just after they left Mary daughter of Marcus, girlfriend of Adam came over. "Where's Brutus going with hairy Mary". "haha what did you call her" laughed Socks. "Hairy Mary" replied Mary. "Thats what she is known as, due to the fact that she has slept with half the guys in the village". "hahaha" all the guys were pissing themselves. "I can't wait to Brutus comes back with another of his alpha male shagging stories" said Dave.

"Boys, we are going to have some fun tonight". Mary brought over a couple of her girlfriends to meet the guys, they were both lovely & had been at the gig. "Is this your first time seeing male strippers" Socks asked the girls. "Hell no" said Laura, "I used to work in London for three years & I saw plenty", "I saw some dance troupe once in Edinburgh" said Angela. "Yeah what were they called" asked Levi. "Oh I don't remember" said Angela "G-Force" said Levi. "can't remember" replied Angela "but they were pretty good". "So you both got boyfriends" asked Hero. "Laura looked at Angela & smiled", "no were both single girls, why", "oh just wondered" replied Hero smiling at the others guys. "Levi do you want to dance" asked Angela as the band done a version of Shania Twains "feel like a woman", "this is my favourite song". "Sure thing" replied Levi. So that was Brutus sorted & Levi sorted. Socks, Hero, Dog & Dave all looked at each other as Laura sat nursing her Bacardi breezer in her hands. Who was going to be the desperado, who was going to make the first move. Don't get me wrong she was a lovely looking girl in a kinda girl next door kinda way. Short brown hair, big blue eyes, with a small dimple on her chin which was amazingly sexy & a great smile. Pretty small tits though. Ah well you couldn't have everything. "So Laura" said Socks "fancy a dance", "Yes that would be lovely" replied Laura. As soon as they went for a dance, Hero turned to the guys "I was just about to ask her, the desperado bastard", "hahaha" laughed the guys. "Well Hero my old cocker spaniel, if your not fast your last" laughed Dog.

The night was kicking on and the guys were getting very pissed. "Is there no curfew in this place, it's 2.15am & the bars still open" said Hero. "Must be because the club is upstairs, the bar will be attached to the club licence" said Dave. "Jesus, look who the cat dragged in" shouted Dog pointing at Brutus as he appeared through the door. "What you been doing mate" sniggered Socks, "what you laughing at you drunkin bums" said Brutus. "Nothing mate, nothing at all" laughed Hero. "Yeah where's your new girlfriend man" said Dave. "She's away up the road, she didn't feel like coming back for a drink", "wonder why not" laughed Socks. Laura and Mary came back to the table with more drinks "Hi Brutus, where's hairy Mary" asked Laura. "Eh, whit" replied Brutus, "what you mean hairy Mary", "hahaha" everybody was now pissing themselves.

3.30 am came & everybody had left apart from Dog, Hero & Dave. Socks & Levi had buggered off with

Laura, Angela, Mary & Adam. Brutus couldn't take the abuse anymore & had left at 3.15. "I love you guys, you guys are the most important thing in my life man, hic !" slobbered Dog to Hero & Dave. "Shut up ya dick" replied Dave. "Yeah man, yer just talking shite cause yer pissed and we didn't get a ride", "yeah man we are the detritus, we are the leftovers from a night of debauchery, we are three failures who couldn't get our holes in a barrel of fannies" said Dave. "haha" laughed Hero "barrel of fannies, i've not heard that in ages". "I still love you guys man, you guys man, you guys are the best guys ive ever met man, I mean hic ! I really love you guys man, hic I mean man" slobbered Dog in a even more slobbery way. "Shut it you fanny, if you mention love or man one more time, i'll shove that bud glass up yer arse" said Dave, "ooooooooooohhhh kinky" laughed Dog, "Love, love, love, love. man, man, man, man" shouted Dog in Daves face. What ensued cannot be printed because it's too kinky so just use your imagination reader !

The following morning the guys were all sitting in the same position as they had been 24 hours earlier. Another bloody choppy day, sitting in another bloody ferry, sitting in the same bloody restaurant, sipping on cups of coffee. They were quiet, hung-over & tired.

Socks turned to the guys & placed his hands under his chin, "anybody want to go and count some Shetland wool jumpers".

Thirteen

The Islands Tour (Part 2)

"Stornoway, bloody Stornoway" shouted Brutus down the phone at Trish. "More like bloody Storm-away, all you get up there is storms & witches burned on a daily basis. It's like a bloody scene out of the Wicker Man" scowled Brutus down the phone again. "Listen Brutus, I have been speaking to this chap Billy on the phone who is hiring you & he is taking a big risk hiring you guys, he has just bought over the only nightclub they have got on the Island & when the locals heard that he was bringing male strippers over, he had a small scale riot on his hands" replied Trish. "Why's that then Trish girl" asked Brutus. "Well seemingly the We Three's still have a lot of power up there", "Aye I bet they do" injected Brutus. "Well, they are none too pleased at his plans, so don't expect a warm reception when you arrive". "You not coming you shitebag" laughed Brutus. "Eh no, I'm too busy with the bands at the moment", "Aye I bet you are" jeered Brutus. "Yeah and also, how come these bloody Islands tours are always in the winter, what's that all about", Trish laughed "Yeah that's right, they do always seem to be at this time of year don't they, better get the thermal undies packed then Brutus".

"Big box small box cardboard box" said Socks doing the box dance as he was driving. "Gonnae keep yer bloody hands on the steering wheel ya maniac" frowned Dave. "Listen you it was your idea to put on the Tony De Vit mix", "therefore it's your fault that I'm doing the box dance", "right then I'll put on Neil Diamond if that'll get you to sit still" said Dave. "No chance I looooooove Neil Diamond, sweet Caroline, good times never seen so good", "save me from imbeciles" retorted Dave.

The guys were in two cars speeding towards Ullapool, where they would then get the ferry over to Stornoway. Now I don't know if you've ever driven to Inverness before ? but if you have then Ullapool is another one hours drive after that. So you are talking four and a half or five hours drive to get there. Straight up to Perth then you hang a right and it is a straight road after that. Unfortunately for about half the way it is a single track road, yes that's right caravans, hgv's, Sunday drivers, women drivers ha ! So stress is unavoidable. Dog was driving one brief & Socks the other. Socks was following Dog, not because Socks didn't know where to go but because

Dog was slower than a week in the jail at driving. What made it worse for Dog was that he had Hero in the car with him. "Keep your bloody foot on the accelerator ya plum" frowned Hero, "you drive like Miss Daisy", "I don't know this road you" retorted Dog. "You've not got to know it dafty, it's not as if it is dark, it's broad daylight, put the bloody foot down, at this rate we'll miss the ferry & you'll get your baws toe'd".

Every now and then Socks would get frustrated & would horse it by Dog just to try and get him to speed up. Sometimes it worked, sometimes it didn't. Just after Inverness Socks pulled into a small garage to get a sandwich and a drink. "Jesus Christ you, another hour and we'll be there" said Levi. "can't wait that long dude, my stomachs rumbling" replied Socks. Socks, Dave & Levi were just finishing of their sandwich & throwing the wrapper in the bin when Dog pulled into the car park. "Hello, cheerio" shouted Socks as they pulled out of the garage. Hero gave them the vicky and they continued on into the garage obviously with the similar snack idea in mind. Socks continued on the road rumbling towards Ullapool. They passed a girl and guy thumbing a lift. "Stop and give them a lift man" said Levi, "we've got room". "No way man" replied Socks, "have you never seen the movie, the Hitcher, they are probably both serial killers, they will have knifes the size of that Australian dude, you know Crocodile Dundee & they will cut us limb to limb & eat our liver with Heinz beans or something". "Some imagination" said Dave, "must be scary being you some of the time". So they continued forward, roar roar went the engine, spit spit went the exhaust, trundle trundle went the wheels, fart fart went Levi. "Hoe man your stinking" said Dave turning his window down. "Yeah man, you shouldn't have had that turkey & stuffing sandwich, it's not even Xmas yet man & your eating turkey" said Socks. "Oh sorrrryyyyyy" said Levi, "I didn't realise that there was a rule book saying that you could only eat turkey at Xmas", "I mean lock me up in the Tower for eating Turkey outwith the silly season".

"Jesus" said Dog to Hero back in car number two as they rolled by the two hitchers "maybe we should give these two poor bastards a lift". "Are you crazy man" replied Hero, "have you never seen that movie Breakdown with Kurt Russell", "yeah I have actually" replied Dog, "and there was no hitch-hikers in it", "Oh your right, thinking of the wrong movie". "I'll tell you this man" said Dog, "I thought that the drive between Aberdeen & Inverness was a barren waistland full off much barren-ness but this takes the biscuit man", "Yeah" said Hero, "this would give a barren waistland a bad name", "I mean there is f**k all, not even the odd cottage here and there, just bloody grass & hills & the odd sheep & burn", "yip I would'nt want to breakdown around here" said Dog, "there's not another car in sight & we haven't seen one since we left that garage". "I wonder how much further ahead these fuds are" said Hero "and I wished I hadn't mentioned that movie Breakdown now, I'm getting paranoid".

The fuds in the car ahead were having the same conversation about the lack of civilisation. "This is what it will probably be like after Armageddon" said Socks, "hows that" replied Levi. "well you know, not another c**t in sight" said Socks. "Well you know" said Dave, Socks could be right for once. "The bomb has gone off & now this is the after-effect", "hows that" repeated Levi. "Well think about it" said Dave, "these latest bombs they've got they destroy everything, not just human beings, all buildings, shops, homes, structures made out of steel, brick & wood, just obliterated. "Yeah man" said Socks, "and what you've got now is the small pockets of survivors scattered across the lands, they have been affected by the fall-out. So they are like zombies now, these hills could be full of them, and it's getting dark now, this is when they come out & when they come out they need to feed", "yeah yeah" said Levi I know where this is heading "your now going to say that they eat flesh & they will spring out in front of us & devour our warm flesh". "Eh I think you have been watching too many films mate" said Socks, "whit, that's calling the kettle black, nobody watches more movies than you ya weirdo" laughed Levi. "No Socks is right Levi", "It is commonly misunderstood that zombies live of human flesh" said Dave, "what they actually eat is far more sinister", "what's that then" asked Levi "dare I ask", "Dandelions" replied Socks, "Dandelions" chortled Levi, "yes dandelions" said Dave, "it is a common mistake to think that zombies are carnivorous", "that's right" said Socks, "dandelions provide all the proper nutrients that Zombies require to remain undead".

"What do you think the guys are talking about" Dog asked Hero. "Who gives a shit, will you put the bloody foot down or let me drive" replied Hero. "It's my car" said Dog, "No way are you driving", "Do I ask to drive your car", "you don't have to" retorted Hero "I don't take a bloody week to get there".

"Are we there yet" shouted Levi from the back seat. "Don't start that crap" laughed Socks.

"Wonder what the guys are talking about" said Dave. "Probably the same as us, zombies" said Socks. "Look" shouted Dave, "the sea", "we're nearly at Ullapool"

"Are we there yet" shouted Levi from the back seat.

Fourteen

The Islands Tour (Part 2 cont'd)

Hester sat across from her pal Marsie in Tinderbox coffee shot in Byres Rd in the West End of Glasgow. The story goes that the Italian dude that owns Tinderbox had been in Glasgow on business, most of it being in the West End. He was appalled that he couldn't get a "decent" cup of coffee in Byres rd. So when he eventually moved to Glasgow, Tinderbox was born. It probably sells the most lethal mocha in Glasgow. Have one of them at lunchtime & you will be rattling for the rest of the afternoon.

Hester sipped on hers while Marsie opted for a green tea. "So where is Socks again" asked Marsie. "Stornoway" replied Hester. Left at 2pm this afternoon back early evening tomorrow. Socks & Hester had been an item for a while now. Marsie had been against them getting together at first because Socks was a stripper. On meeting him though she had immediately liked him & had also met all the other guys. "bleedin Stornoway" said Marise, "you can't get much further away than that", "tell me about it" said Hester. "Do you trust him when he is away with the rest of the Guys like that, you know staying in a hotel overnight, getting drunk in the company of women", "Yes, I mainly trust him, don't get me wrong I do have an element of doubt sometimes, but I suppose that is only natural" replied Hester. "I am usually a pretty good judge of character & yes I would say that he is faithfull & Connor loves him to death & Socks is so good with him". "How is the little darling doing" said Marsie, "turning into a little man, getting very cheeky" laughed Hester. "Fancy another Mocha" enquired Marsie. "No way, I am buzzing already on this one, I'll take a tea though and a slice of carrot cake if you are buying", "coming right up" said Marsie.

Hester sat and stared at the people bustling along Byres rd going about their daily toil. There couldn't be anywhere else in Glasgow that you saw so many cultures from all over the World all congregated in one place. The University was just around the corner, so half of them would be going there. Half of the people were students in the west end. It had a great student culture, fantastic nightlife. She had really changed and developed as a person since leaving Dunoon. It was the best thing she could have done.

Marsie returned with two cups of green tea & two slices of carrot cake. Yummy. They sat outside & were the only two doing so. Who cared they were wrapped up to the max, scarfs, hats, the full nine yards. It had been a busy afternoon xmas shopping up the town & this was there wee relaxing treat at the end of it. Hester sipped her tea & stared at the sea of traffic & heads bobbing up and down going to and fro on Byres Rd.

Socks sipped his pint & watched the sea get choppier & choppier. "If the bleedin weather conditions don't pick up, we won't be going anywhere" complained Socks. The barman overheard what Socks said, "don't worry, it has to be a hell of a lot worse than this for them to cancel the sailing". "What gale force 9 rather than gale force 8" replied Socks. "Don't be such a drama queen old Socky boy" said Brutus. "Hows Hester doing these days the Sockster" asked Hero, "aye fine bro, she's away out shopping today in Glasgow with the Marsie girl". "Is that Marsie still single" enquired Levi, "No" laughed Socks, "she met some dude a few weeks back & is loved up already". "Damn" said Levi, "I should have made my move before now", "you've got no chance boy, I've already warned her about you", "why, cheers mate, I knew there was a reason I didn't like you"

At 5pm they got their arses in gear & made there way down to the ship or boat or whatever your meant to call it. Once they were settled once again in there favourite place, yes the restaurant. Socks asked the question. "Is this a ship or a boat", Who cares, does it matter" replied Brutus. "Yeah it matters" said Socks. "I think it is to do with the size of the vessel" said Dave. "Oh er Matron" laughed Hero, "leave my vessel out of it". "Yeah I think Dave is right" perked up Dog. "Yeah ok" said Socks, "I'll take that onboard", "oh get it onboard" laughed Socks at his own crap joke. "For instance" said Dave, "you talk about sailing boats don't you, you know the type, your typical well off geezer who has a twenty-five foot sailing boat & goes out in it wearing a daft wee captains hat", "Yeah and he calls it something like Lucile after his Missus or something", "So what about say a tug that escorts the big bad boys out to sea or brings them back in" said Socks. "Well you've just answered that haven't you dafty, its a bleeding tug" said Brutus. "as for the lovely Caledonian Macbrayne that takes you to Dunoon or Rothesay or in our case Stornoway, well that's a ship" said Dog. "So in that case the P & O or Stena Line ferries are bloody big ships then" laughed Socks. "As for the Navy, they have warships don't they" said Dog, "it would sound bloody silly if you said warboats wouldn't it" "I am so glad you monkeys cleared that up, can we please get down to the important business now" said Hero, "who wants the fish & who wants the steak pie".

"I think I'll have the spaghetti carbonara please" said Hester to the waiter, "i'll have the pepperoni pizza" said Marsie. They had moved on from the West End over to the Quay, they had dumped the shopping in the boot of the car & were now dining in Frankie & Benny's. Then they were off to the Cinema to bring to an end a lovely day. "I love the carbonara in here" said Hester. "A waiter told me once that it is the one dish that they get for free, so all the staff always choose it", "why's that then" enquired Marsie. "Well seemingly because it is such a popular dish they make a big massive pot of it", "nice one" said Marsie. "Sooo Hester darling, there is something I'm dying to ask you", "shoot" replied Hester. "Well have you and Socky boy done it yet", "Marsssssie", "I'll take that as a yes will I" laughed Marsie. "none of your business Marsie and I'm surprised at you asking me" said Hester with a glint in her eye. "It's just that, well, I, well, I wondered if he had a big one or not" said Marsie. Hester burst out laughing, "well he is a male stripper Marsie, what do you think".

"So Socks man" said Hero, "have you and Hester shagged yet", all the guys burst out laughing. "None of your bloody business you cheeky git" scowled Socks. "That means no" chortled Hero. "Listen Hester is special, she is different from the rest of the birds I have been with in every way, especially because of her strict upbringing" said Socks."Listen dude I didn't ask for a history lesson, I just asked you if you had shagged her" said Hero cheekily. Socks got up, "I'm going for some fresh, anybody coming", "yeah" said Dave. The Guys watched Socks & Dave head of for the upper deck. "Think you hit a raw nerve there Hero man" said Levi. "How much longer in this tin can" enquired Brutus. "why you feeling sqweezy" asked Hero. "Another hour and a half" said Levi.

The "ship" pulled into Stornoway harbour at just after 7.30pm and Billy was waiting for them in his Vauxhall Frontera 4 x 4. He was a middle aged guy with a mop of greying hair & the same colour of beard. They were only in the car for two minutes and they were at the hotel where they were staying further along the harbour. It was pitch black & the guys could only see the hotel by the lights that were on. For some reason there was no street lights. Looks like somebody hadn't paid their council tax. The Guys had to be at the club for 9.30 to start for 10pm, so they just had time to go in & clean up & grab a change of clothes, in Hero's case, a fresh pair of black jeans & a black t-shirt. In Socks case a fresh pair of combats & a white t-shirt. They then headed down to the hotel bar for the last three quarters of an hour to get more "relaxed" before they headed out. There was two barmaids, both young and both attractive in their own ways. One was a goth & had loads of piercings in her face & the other was the opposite, very prim & proper looking.

Billy arrived back at the same time the guys got to the bar. Good timing he could get the drinks in, which he did, good lad. He explained to them how he had been frightened driving through the town for the last two weeks because he was expecting somebody to take a pot shot at him. "That's right" said Dave, I half expected the We Three's to be waiting for us with placards on the pier". "Don't laugh" said Billy the night is but young, I wouldn't be surprised if they will be waiting outside the club. "Doubt it" said Gloria the goth barmaid, "They'll be in bed by then". The Guys all laughed. "Is it really that bad here" asked Socks. "Well put it this way" replied Billy, "I was refused a Sunday licence for the club because of the pressure that they applied to the board". "The thing is" continued Billy, I am not a pure bred Islander, I only moved over here from Aberdeen two years ago to take the club over plus this hotel", "so I will never be accepted by the pure bred Islanders and the fact that I am a devil worshiping nightclub owner spreading sin with my evil dance music & now strippers, I'm just doomed". Socks thought twice about asking for a shot on the decks. Sounded like he was in enough trouble without going there.

Billy headed off to open the club, he was coming back in twenty minutes to get the guys. Dog thought to himself if Billy would go out and check under his car for any strange looking devices before starting the engine haha. The guys sat and chatted to the barmaids until Billy returned. They were the only ones in the bar. Was that strange ? Both the barmaids were eighteen & were pure born & bred Stornoway. They were your usual bored teenagers, dying to get of the Island at the first possible opportunity. Gloria was going to college in Inverness to do a course in Hotel Marketing. Sharon was going to Benidorm with another Stornoway friend to work in a bar for the season next year & it would be the longest time she will have been off the Island.

The gig was well busy. It wasn't a big club but there was at least eighty chicks rammed into it. They were actually quite trendy for Islanders. They responded well to everything the guys done & were a bit radio rental. Totally different to the Mull gig, night and day. At the end of the gig they were all asking for autographs. "I feel like Fake That" said Hero. It was a great soundsytem as well, which always helps & buzzes up the crowd with better effect. The guys headed back to their hotel at the end of the night, they didn't bother waiting on Billy. It was only two minuted walk with the bags, so no big deal. The word had got out where they were staying (small town) and there was about twenty of the girls in the hotel bar from the gig. The locals had also came out (must start late on Stornoway) and the bar was packed. The guys dumped their bags in their rooms & headed back down to the bar for some serious drinking. Billy appeared with a big beaming face. The night had gone well & he had not been shot or blown up - yet !

The following morning Socks threw open his curtains & gasped. He knew he was on the harbour but hadn't realised how close. There was a road right outside his bedroom window, then a wall, then the sea. There was a "tug" bobbing up and down right in front of him, big tyres tied to it side, bouncing of massive tyres tied to the pier wall, further out from the harbour was a big lighthouse painted red & white. It looked very romantic & majestic sitting there as the sea lapped on the side of it's walls. How long had it stood there protecting the ships from a watery grave, how much longer will it. Socks boiled the kettle and made a cup of Joe, he felt ok, he hadn't overdone it on the booze the previous night. He was getting older & was calming down. The other guys were the same, they didn't really talk about it, just carried on as normal, but they all knew it. They had been doing this game a long time now. Socks sat on the edge of the bed & sipped on his coffee. He stared at the wonderful view & thought about Hester.

Fifteen

Hester was pacing up and down (as people who pace normally do) in her bedroom. She was fuming. Her fists were clenched & her faced contorted with anger. She kicked the bed. The bed had done nothing to Hester to receive this unwanted act of violence, but it was the nearest thing to her at that point in time. "How dare he talk to me like that", "who the hell does he think he is", "I have had enough of this shit". All of the above thoughts raced through Hester's brain.

Rewind four hours. Connor son of Hester was getting ready to leave to go to school. It was 6.30pm & he was in the school play. It was called "Everybody Out" and was a satire about the life of Hitler before he became a murdering genocide dictator. Back in the days when he was humble painter with strong political ramblings. Bit of a strange choice for a school play you may think. Well Connor went to a public school, Hutcheson Primary over in the Southside of Glasgow. The "posh" part. So I suppose what with the fees that the parents have to pay, that "Annie get your gun" and "Carousel" might seem a bit low key. Hester was trying to get him out the door as he was running late and the play was kicking of at 7.30 & he had to get into costume. Socks was sitting patiently in the car waiting to drive them to the school. "C'mon you two, I want to get a good seat" shouted Socks sarcastically. "Keep your hair on dafty, we'll just be a minute" retorted Hester.

The play kicked of about five minutes late & it was a full house. Connor just had a small part, well he was only seven years old. The play went well though & the audience was in good spirits, probably because it was finished & they could shoot up the road. On the way out Hester was talking to some of the other Mothers & Socks was kicking his feet impatiently holding Connor's hand waiting for her to hurry up. He got a tap on the shoulder & turned to see one of his mate's ex's from years back. "Tracy honey, how the hell are you gal" enquired Socks, giving Tracy a peck on the cheek and a cuddle. "I'm fine doll" replied Tracy, "what the hell is a wido like you doing here", "very funny you" replied Socks, "my girlfriends wee boy, Connor here goes to the school & was in the play", "Hi Connor" said Tracy, waving down at the wee chap, "Hi" said Connor shyly. "My friends wee boy goes to Hutchy and I'm just here for a bit of moral support" said Tracy. "How's Jim these days" asked Tracy about her ex and Socks mate. "Not sure doll, I've not seen him in about eight or nine months. I know that he had moved house and got engaged". "Yeah I heard that news" said Tracy. Socks turned to Hester, "Hester this is an old friend from back in the day, Tracy", "Oh so what are you talking to me now then" said Hester looking raging. She then turned her back to him. Socks just looked at her in disbelief & then turned to Tracy, "sorry Tracy I've got to go" and gave her a peck on the cheek. Tracy just looked totally embarrassed. Socks strode of dragging Connor behind him. Hester arrived at the car two minutes later and they drove home in silence. When they got back to the house Socks made Connor some milk & biscuits & told him to get into his jammies. Socks then read him a bedtime story. When he got back downstairs, Hester was sitting smoking and watching some programme about house diy. "Do you want a coffee" Socks asked Hester coldly, "no thanks" she replied even more coldly. Socks made himself one & came back into the room & sat on the other couch. "What was that all about" he enquired. "nothing" answered Hester, not making eye contact with him. "Well it must have been about something or you wouldn't have acted like such a rocket" Socks retorted. Hester throw him a glare, she hated that word. "Did you just kick of because I was talking to another female" enquired Socks. "You just totally ignored me, you turned your back to me & totally cut me off" Hester injected. "What" replied Socks in disbelief. "You weren't even talking to me you were to talking to the milf's and your back was turned to me dafty". "Oh whatever Socks, if that's what you want to think then you must be right", said Hester fuming. "I tell you what Hester, you had better never embarrass me like that again ok" said Socks feeling the anger rise inside him. Hester stormed out of the room. Socks sat and stared blankly into the wall beside the fireplace. This hadn't been the first time that Hester had displayed challenging behaviour. She would frequently spit the dummy out the pram over one thing or the other. The thing was that she was a green eyed monster. The fact that Socks was a stripper definitely fueled the fires. Socks knew that it couldn't be easy going out with somebody that was in his line of business. Trust was major quality that was needed. The thing was with Hester, Socks new that it wouldn't have mattered if he had been a bus driver, she still wouldn't trust him.

*Reverse the scenario. How would Socks react if the shoe was on the other foot (*never really understood that wee quirp, obviously the shoe wouldn't fit the other foot because it would be the right on the left or the left on the right.....yeah *!, oh hold on I think I get it now - doh !). How would he react if Hester's occupation was a "garment removing technician". How would he feel if Hester was getting her Bristol Cities & chicken biriani out on a regular basis. A group of guys standing silently with their right arms raised in a masonic handshake, pint gripped sweaty in their palms. Nudging each other in a alpha-male, peer pressure is a bitch like ritual. "check out the tits on her big man", "shit man, look at that ass, what I would do to that ass man". Even worse, escorting Hester to the gigs and being approached by the scumbugs, "hey mate, does Candy Cane do extras", "awright chief, does that Candy Cane bird do blow jobs". Aaaaaaaaah !! I am staying in for a night of babysitting with the Connster and Candy Cane ahem I mean Hester is heading out for a bit of garment removal. The wee guy is piled of to bed at 10 bells and I am sitting by MYSELF just thinking about that particular pastime that Hester is up to. My mind is working overtime, who is she speaking to, what is she saying, does she fancy any of the guys, do they fancy her (*stupid question, cancel that*), is she considering leaving with anybody, will she be later than usual coming home. The paranoid android would be working overtime. Now being a Male Stripper Socks I am sure would like to think that he would not be hypocritical enough to think or worse act that way. I would like to think that he would say to himself, hey I am doing the same job (but with different tools) and I know she trusts me, afterall I come home to her every night. So therefore I will trust her with the same integrity that she offers me. "Hi baby how was your gig", "fine darling, a couple of guys grabbed my tits and* *one kept slapping my arse, but apart from that it was fine babes", "really darling, glad to hear it, sounds like you had a smashing night". Right, WRONG. "whaaaaaaaat, whyyyyyyy the Mutherf**kers, i'll f**king kill the assholes, then their whole families, then myself rather than serving ten consecutive life sentences".*

Reader, are you in a similar predicament? Is your partner a male or female stripper ? Help is at hand. Don't suffer alone. Log onto "www.mylifeisruinedbymyassholestrippingpartnerandIneedhelpquick.com". Leave us your views and receive a free g-string worth $6.99.

Then there's the other sticky subject with Hester. "We never have anybody around at the weekend for a meal because your always gigging", "I am very sorry that my job, that I love, interferes with your tea parties", "We never go out because you are always gigging at the weekend", "not true, we go out midweek or on a Sunday". Two pieces of advice for any budding male strippers out there who want to be male strippers but also have hankerings over being in a relationship. One, if your better half gives you plenty of notice about some family thingy, whether it be a wedding, a fortieth birthday party, a day at the races, whatever it is, put it in your diary in big bold letters and make sure that you don't take a gig, because if you do, she will cast it up to you for eternity. Two, if you make plans to go on holiday, do not, I repeat, do not come back to do a gig and then return to the holiday. Not only will she cast it up to eternity she will chase you down to hell and make sure the horned one also casts it up, the beeatch.

Hester was on the phone to Linda. "Hi Babes, how do you fancy a cheeky wee night out with Socks & one of his buddy's next weekend", "Yeah honey, that would be nice, what is his mate like" replied Linda. "He's a good looking guy, very athletic, quite a nice guy with it as well, his name is Evano", "What is he Italian" said Linda, "No he's from Springburn" laughed Hester. "Where are we off to babes" laughed Linda, "well how about starting at mines for a couple of drinks then heading over to Sauchiehall St for a couple of bars then finish up in Vicky's Nightclub for a dance round the handbag. "Sounds like a plan doll, so is this Evano guy single then" said Linda, "off course babes, that's why I am trying to fix you up" laughed Hester again.

The weekend in question arrived and Linda & Evano arrive at Hester's gaff for drinky poo's (sorry, that sounded very camp). Socks was already there. Fast forward brrrrrrrrrrr brrrrrrrrrrr brrrrrrrrrrrrrrr, in the town having more drinky poo's, fast forward brrrrrrrrr brrrrrrrrrr brrrrrrrrrrrr, in the Savoy Nightclub (very very cheesy nightclub in Glasgow City Centre, but a good laugh all the same), fast forward brrrrrrr brrrrrrrr brrrrrrrrr brrrrrrrrr (I gave it one more brrrrrrrrr there because I was feeling fiesty), outside said cheesy Nightclub. Hester is sulking in a doorway and ignoring Socks, "what's up honeybunny" Socks enquired as Linda and Evano huddled together beside him (they had hit it off), "don't you what's up me" said Hester. Socks had that feeling again, you know the one, the OH NO, HERE WE GO AGAIN FEELING. "Whatever do you mean sweetness" asked Socks with a feeling of woe. "You ignored me nearly the whole evening, you only danced with me once & hardly bought me a drink all night and too cap it all you get talking to these two girls", "oh is that all" thought Socks to himself but was too much of a shitebag to say it out loud. "What are you rambling on about dafty, I was talking to you most of the night, I bought you loads of drinks, I asked the DJ to play your favourite choon, Shania Twain & I only spoke to these two birds for five minutes max". "Eh Hester, Evano and me are going to shoot babes, eh we are going back to mines, eh so eh I'll see you later ok babes, phone me, love you !!", Linda looked at Hester who was just standing hugging herself in the doorway, looking at the ground in between glaring at Socks and just ignored Linda. Evano was looking very forlorne & just shrugged his shoulders at Socks & Linda and him headed of for a night of steamy sex, toys and all. The only steamy situation that Socks was going to enjoy that night was getting out of one. Two minutes passed with Hester & Socks not saying a word to each other. Eventually Hester just pushed by Socks and started striding up Sauchiehall street. Socks hesitated for a moment just staring after her, then he made off after her. "Slow down Hester, listen I'm sorry ok, please just slow down and talk to me", "are you really sorry or are you just saying that" said Hester suddenly drawing to a halt. "Of course I mean it, I wouldn't say it unless I mean it" replied Socks lying. He didn't mean it at all, he hadn't done anything wrong, in fact if anybody should be apologising it should be Hester. Men of the World, we all know this is the way it should be BUT we also know that it will never be that way, not until the World freezes over or hell or both. Why ? well because men like to live a quiet simple life & women, well, women like to live in a soap opera, full stop. So Socks lied and Hester instantly forgave him and came up and gave him a cuddle & they started heading down Sauchiehall street again arm in arm. Happy ending ? Happy families ? Fence mended ? Yes ? No ! Socks was walking along entwined in his better half. He was biting his lip, no don't say anything, Socks don't say anything, Socks. "You know you can act like a right idiot at times" He said while still cuddling Hester. WHAM BANG WALLOP, World War three, aaaaahhhhh ! Hester is striding out once again heading down Sauchiehall street making for Charing Cross. "I'm sorry, I didn't mean it" Socks is shouting after her, still standing still after his bombshell comment. People were walking by & staring at him. Clubbers & party-goers heading home. Hester was still striding and Socks was still standing. F**k !! Socks started running to catch her up. "Babes slow down, you know I love you", ignored, "Babes slown down, you know I would do anything for you" still ignored. Hester was a steam train, choo choo, clippity cloppity clippity cloppity went the diamonte high heel size five shiny red shoes out Morgans. Her long black hair trailed behind her like a turbo Vidal Sasoon hairdryer was attached with scaffolding to the front of her napper. She branched onto the junction at Charing Cross & headed of Sauchiehall street making for Bath Street. Socks wasn't far behind, his eyes were trans-fixed to the target. "Babes, slow down, I'm getting a stitch with all that lager, babes", ignored & ignored once again. The matching double clasped leather red handbag with triple strap was tucked under the arm like a Sergeant Major's baton, hup one two three four, your in the Hester McCready Marine Core. The red sequenced body hugging dress was getting tested to the limit, the lovely acorn shaped buttocks were bouncing inside the flimsy material, bounce bounce bounce, right buttock bounce to the left, left buttock bounce to the right. It could be a popular commercial pop song down your local on a Friday night. Friday night is karaoke night. "Whose up for the buttock bounce song" yells the presenter over the mic. Bounce to the left.

Bounce bounce bounce and bounce again.

She was making a b-line by the Mitchell library, Glasgow biggest and most famous library adored and hated by students in equal amounts as exam day approached. Bounce bounce. "Babes slow down, I love you so much". Socks ran by a couple snogging at the back of the library. They seemed to get a fright, Socks couldn't care less. Jesus she had great calves, not the bird in the doorway, Hester, yip Hester had great calves. The sort of calves that looked great in anything, red sequenced dress's, cycling shorts, short bath robes, Mmmmm short bath robes. Had he ever told her. Couldn't remember. He would tell her, he would tell her right now. "Babes slow down, I think you have got great calves, especially when you are running, it accentuates the the diamond shape of the muscle even more, I love your calves. I know you love diamonds but I love your calves". What was that about diamonds, was that a tie in. Why did I even mention diamonds. Jesus she'll think that I am going to get her a diamond or three now, stupid asshole, don't mention diamonds again. Had she heard, she didn't seem to have. The steam train was still gaining speed. She had made it down to Saint Vincent street and was passing by the high flats where she used to live. I only had two minutes to catch her then it would be too late, mission failed. Another lonely night in my own scratcher, scratch scratch, aaaah. "Babes slow down, I love you more than you could know". SLAM, went the front door to her tenement. It was electronically operated by a key fob. I was not the proud owner of one. Give her a minute to get upstairs, she lives on the top landing. I could hear her footsteps getting fainter. CLIPPITY CLOPPITY clippity cloppity clip. Search through handbag for keys, can't find keys, empty contents of handbag on the floor outside her front door, rummage rummage, find keys, keys in door, door open. BUZZ BUZZ. Ignored, again ! buzz buzz, "babes let me in", ignored, "babes" ignored, "babes are you there, it's freezing out here" ignored, "babes". F**K IT. Taxi, home, shoes off, dimmed light in living room, cup of coffee, two digestive biscuits. Sulk, more sulking, some more sulking, rocket, bunny boiler, rocket bunny boiler. She had a problem, she needs professional help. Is it my fault. What if it's all my fault. Maybe it's me that's the rocket (scientist), maybe it's me that's the bunny boiler (the male version). Maybe I should give up the stripping, f**k that, that's how she met me, I've never hidden it from her. Maybe I should though, do I love her enough to give it up. Yeah I f**king love her enough, I bloody worship the ground she walks on, no denying it, I have it bad, a bad case of love sickness, no known cure to man nor beast. I'm a selfish c**t though, I want my cake and I want to eat it. Go to bed, everything will seem clearer, better in the morning. Have two more digestive biscuits, a cup of tea, brush my teeth, brusha brusha brusha. Wash my face, do a pee. Strip of (without music) and climb into my scratcher, Zzzzzz, dreaming, rocket bunny boiler.

Ring ring, ring ring. "Hello", Socks

sleepily answers the phone. "Hi it's me" Hester voice informed him. "What time is it" enquired Socks. "Ten o'clock". "Listen I didn't mean for you to go home last night, I was just about to let you in when you buggered off". "Have you had breakfast yet" asked Socks. "No I was too upset to eat". "Why don't I bring some in and we can have it in bed". "That would be lovely, I get Connor back at three, can you come over soon". "Yeah I'll just jump into the shower and I'll be over". "Socks". "Yes Hester". "Just step into the shower, don't jump in case you slip and bang that stupid head of yours". "Haha very funny dafty, see you soon". Socks hung up and smiled, result, a bit of brekkie in bed and then some good making up sex, you can't whack it. Then he frowned, this was only a reprieve and he knew it. This had been happening a lot. They had already split up twice and then got back together, third time lucky ? Socks knew that this was make or break time. Something had to be done and soon. God he really loved her so much & didn't want to lose her. So old Socky boy started thinking a certain way. His thought process changed. Socks started thinking about diamonds.

Sixteen

Two months passed, the situation had not improved. They had been bickering about that, bickering about this. The funny thing was, if any of Socks mates asked him what they had been fighting about, he couldn't remember. The same scenario with Hester, she couldn't recall either. One thing was for sure though, it was Hester who usually started it. Then things came to a head and I don't mean a wee small napper I mean an all out guns blazing apocalypse. Socks & Hero had been booked for a two man show in sunny Clydebank (Socks home Town) in Shoot Soccer. Hester has asked is he minded if her & a good friend Deirdrie from Campbletown came along. "No worries babes" Socks had said. He was to regret that big time.

Well without kicking the arse out of the story, the summary is that one of Socks ex workmates from a full time jobbie had been there with some friends. Well the drink was flowing and The ex workmate Amber decided to gate crash the changing area that Socks and Hero was in. The major thing that Socks done wrong was letting them. He should have screwed the nut on that one right there with "sorry girls, no audience allowed in the changing area", now I know it sounds wanky but he should have said it rather than "awright girls come on in, Amber how you doing doll, i've not seen you in ages". Well quite rightly so Hester took exception to this and was more than vocal to it to Socks when the Girls had vacated the area. Unfortunately they seemed to get the jest of what was going on and being Drumchapel ladies decided that they were having none of it. So there was a situation with a bottle of lime flavoured Bacardi Breezer getting aimed at Hester's head. Now anybody that knows Hester pretty well will vouch that she prefers said BB down her throat and not over her napper. So a certain Male Stripper named Socks had to intervene and removed said BB from said female and then escort her from the changing area.

So as you can imagine World War three erupted once again and the diplomatic skills had to be put into place. "So Deirdrie did you enjoy the gig" Hero enquired. "Eh yeah thanks Hero it was fine" answered Deirdrie politely. "Shut up Hero" shouted Hester not amused. "Don't take it out on him babes" interrupted Socks. "That's right you stick by your mate, you two are as thick as thieves" screamed Hester. "Now Hester I don't think" started Hero. "Hero don't say a word mate" said Socks cutting him off. "Socks I want to go home" Hester shouted. "Ok ok I've just got to get squared up with the money first", "it's ok bro you guys get the car packed up & I'll get the cash sorted" interrupted Hero. Red light, stop, amber, get ready, green light, "that's it Socks, I can't take any more, that's the last straw, I haven't been in a fight since school" sobbed Hester. The tears were running down her face and bouncing of her hair-piece. Hester would wear a long false hair extension from time to time. It was actually very life like and convincing and a lot of people thought that it was the real thing. At this point in time one half was caught up and wrapped round the seatbelt like a hairy snake bobbing up and down now and again as the car went over bumps in the road and swaying to the left and the right as the erratic driver took corners too fast. The snake "Socrates" wasn't saying anything. Hester wasn't just upset and crying, she was angry as well & an upset, crying, angry Hester is not a good combination. "Why oh why oh why did I let these tarts into the changing room" thought Socks. "No more Socks, just, just no more ok, you will have to make a decision what you want, the Highlanders or me, because you can't have both anymore, ok, you just can't have both, I am sick to the back teeth of playing second fiddle to you and your stripper mates" rant rant, rant some more. Socrates was still sitting not saying anything. "How would you like it if I was a stripper", "I wouldn't" thought Socks. "Eh, well, how would you like it, well, if I brought you to gigs", "aye right" thought Socks, "well, how would you like it if I brought guys into the changing room", "eh well Hester I haven't given it much thought" said Socks, for the first time speaking since he got in the car. "Socks, don't interrupt me when i'm ranting, I mean speaking" said Hester annoyed. "Well how would you like it, guys in the changing room, me with my tits out for all the world to see", "it's hardly the world babes, just the changing room" said Socks humbly. "Humour, was that humour, well, was it". "Raindrops keep falling on my head" the singer on Real radio FM belted out over the speakers. "Socks, change that bloody station, I'm not in the mood for raindrops", bzzzzz bzzzzz whirl bzzzzzz bzzzzz eech eech bzzzzzz, "it's raining men hallelujah, it's raining men" not that either, bzzzzz bzzzzz bzzzzzz eech "I'm a male stripper in a gogo bar, strip for me babe strip for you", "aaaaaahhhhhh" screamed Hester. Socks turned to her as he was driving and burst out laughing. He looked at her tear stained face. She just stared back at him, "It's not funny Socks, it's really not funny at all, not one little bit". Socks held up his left hand and made a tiny wee size with his thumb and forefinger. "Just a tad funny" he smirked. "Just a tinchy winchy little bit funny". He turned the dial on the radio, bzzzzzz bzzzzz whirl eech, "it's going to be a loverly day, a loverrrrrrlllllllyyyyyy day". Hester burst out laughing. "Thankyou FM radio" thought Socks. "Your a bastard, but I still love you" said Hester. "I love you as well babes", "I love you loads".

The making up sex was good, real good. It was true what they said. Sex is so much better with somebody you love or really care about. It's a funny thing that fine line between really liking somebody and loving somebody. When you like somebody, you can be sitting the following morning having breakfast together & say something like "that sex was real good last night, I needed that", but when you love somebody, using the "sex" word just doesn't seem right. It would be "are you ok honey, I was too rough making love last night was I". Or if you are sitting on the couch watching TV together and you are feeling horny. You would say "do you want to go to bed and make love". Although I've never used that line in my life because I think it sounds cheesy as f**k, but I am sure loads of folk use it.

It was the morning after the gig, Socks lay awake staring at Hester as she lay sleeping. He had not slept well. Socks was worried. He knew that they had made up last night but that was only a brief reprieve from the executioner. God she was beautiful, she looked so peaceful when she was sleeping. Her mouth was upturned slightly into small smile, she was having a nice dream, probably about that David Hasslehoff or somebody. Her eyes were twitching gently behind the eyelids and her gorgeous pixie like nose was flaring up and down ever so easy as she breathed. Socks turned back on his back and stared at the ceiling. Something caught his eye over to the right and he made a mental note to brush away that cobweb that had been there the last three months. He sighed heavily, what to do, what to do. He sat up and swang his legs out of bed. He walked bollock into the living room. Damn, living room curtains wide open again. Another heart attack to the neighbours. He walked up to the open window, yawned, stretched, farted and then closed the blinds half over. He scratched his arse and got a tiny bit of crustie jobbie under his fingernail (you know the way you do when you haven't cleaned your bum fully enough). He went to the bathroom to wash his hands (honest !). Made a cup of coffe, good strong coffee with a half sugar & one cow. Made his way back into the living room, scratched his balls and then sat sipping his coffee of much strongness with his legs sprawled over the couch. What to do, what to do. He turned on the TV, an army commercial came on, nope too old and didn't fancy going to war either. He changed channels, a Navy commercial came on, nope, still too old and didn't like being on a boat (or a ship) for any long period of time. The Gourock to Dunoon twenty minute ferry was quite long enough thank you very much. He took a sip of his coffee and changed back to the original channel, a commercial came on advertising for a career as a mechanic. Nope still to old (are you beginning to get the idea), and I am shite with my hands, apart from when I am picking my bum. Took another swig of coffee. Shouldn't really swig coffee, it's more of a sipping drink, aaaaahhh ! burnt mouth, damn. What to do, what to do. I could start my own business, doing what though. I could have independant record shop specialising in dance 12" vinyl. Nope, vinyl is on the way out, cd's & mp3 are taking over. Digital djing is the future. Serato final scratch. Ableton live. Ok so I could start a website selling digital music "DJSocksdownload.com". Would need good start up funds. Nope not got them. Could go to the bank and get a load. Nope not got a great credit history, wouldn't get one. Could try one of these enterprise fund thingy's, nope bollock, wouldn't work. Have to be mega keen to do something like that, nah just not keen enough. How about personal trainer, nope I love going to the gym, that's my down time, that would take away from it if I was there all the time. Supplement Company, nope, same reason as the website sketch, money, keen-ness. I could be a Salesman, nope they have to work long hours and I am a lazy bastard at heart. What to do, what to do. Social Care, shite money, have to go to college first and get a qualification. Nope, shite at studying, don't fancy going back to college either. Saying that I do quite fancy Social Care, there are loads of people out there with problems, I would be good at that job, I know I would. What to do, what to do.

"Socks put some clothes on ya flasher" said Hester entering the room. "Hi Babes, did you sleep well" enquired Socrates. "Not really", "liar" thought Socks. She seemed distant. Socks knew that she was still thinking about the previous night. "Do you want some coffee honey", "please babes". He returned with the coffee to find her crying again. "Whats up hun". "Nothing", "oh nothing eh, doesn't seem like that nothing to me", "are you still upset about last night". "Of course I'm still f**king upset about last night Socrates", "Oh Socrates is it" thought Socks, must be serious. "I just can't go along like this anymore, I just can't handle your occupation anymore, I was serious about what I said last night, it is either me or the stripping Socks, I really mean it". "Babes, you know that I was planning on packing it in when I am forty, there is only three years to go, can you handle it to then" explained Socks bashfully. "Whhhhhhaaaatttttt", explosions, tear gas, scud missiles, m16 rifles, grenades, anti-tank missiles. READERS, *I take it you get the idea.* Hester slams the front door to Socks flat closed five minues later. World record for getting ready thought Socks, why can't she do that normally. Well that didn't go to plan thought Socks. That didn't go too well, not too well at all.

The phone rang, ring ring, ring ring. "Hello" Socks answered, he knew it wouldn't be Hester, too quick. "Awrite me old son" said Hero. "No, not really, in-fact totally shite if you really want to know" replied Socks sarcastically. "Oh dear, that sounds serious, have you been dumped then". "Hero how do you fancy taking me out and cheering me up mate" asked Socks. "No worries dude, let's go to Cafe Nero on hope st, your favourite right", "right" replied Socks. "I'll buy you an Americano" said Hero. "See you in thirty minutes". Socks heard Hero as usual before he saw him. The droan of his 3.0L Brooklands Capri exhaust pricked up Socks ears as it pulled up outside his flat. "Awrite fanny baws" said Hero to Socks, "awrite fudnuts" replied Socks belting himself in. He loved Hero's car. Hero liked to drive fast and this was no exception. The noise from the lifetime guarantee magnatex exhaust was awesome. Magnatex made some of the best exhaust systems in the world. Most Porches sported them. The particular one that was on Hero's Capri set him back £350, but he didn't care. It looked and sounded amazing. He got admiring and envious looks of guys everywhere he drove. Their heads would turn from fifty yards away as the beast approached. Hero's car always cheered Socks up. It was funny how cars had the power to do that. Hero's was one of them. "There you go mate, latest mix cd" said Socks putting the new cd into Hero's glove compartment. "What's it like mate, a bit of Hungarian international trance" laughed Hero. "Funny you should say that" replied Socks, "It's more Albanian rural melodic trance actually". "Har har har" laughed Hero. "That was what I was going to say the first time", "really" laughed Socks.

They parked the car in the underground carpark in Anderson and walked around to Cafe Nero in Hope st. Hero had a mocha and a packet of crisps & Socks had an Americano and crisps. "So my main man pray tell what the goss is" enquired Hero. Socks was staring out of the window sipping on his coffee & not answering. "Socks man, talk to me, is it bad". Socks turned to him and nodded his head. "I think she is going to dump me dude, I really think she has had enough this time". "Take her for a nice meal, take a weekend off, go somewhere nice, spend some money on her, buy her underwear, perfume, flowers". Socks shook his head, these alpha male gestures will not work this time mucker", "are you sure, you could push the boat out and buy her shoes & a handbag".

"Not this time mate, this time desperate measures are needed and they are needed now".

Seventeen

Socks climbed out of bed & looked out of the window. It was a cloudy overcast day. It had been raining earlier but the sun was trying to pierce the clouds but to no avail. Socks hadn't seen Hester for a week. She had spoke to him briefly a couple of times on the phone but the conversation was more than a tad cold. It was Sunday morning and he had been gigging on both Friday & Saturday night. This had a dual purpose of both keeping him busy & his mind of Hester while he was working & making him think of her even more when he arrived back home. His mind wasn't on the gigs at the moment, he knew that his performances were also under par. He had made a decision last night after arriving home from the gig. The decision was made at precisely 1.47am. He needed to phone Hester, he had to see her.

The phone rang, "hi mum, yes I am fine mum, how are you. Yes I am still coming for dinner tomorrow night. I don't know if Hester & Connor are coming, I'll let you know tomorrow. How's dad. Listen mum I need to take care of something now, can I phone you tomorrow. Ok bye". He put the phone back on the cradle. He went to get dressed, white shirt for a change me thinks. Karl Lagerfeld aftershave, nice touch. The phone rang, "Awright fudnuts, how you doing mate, yeah I'm fine mate. Dave can I phone you later I am tied up with something at the moment bro, yeah mate catch you later". Good shoes, these nice brown leather ones. Good watch. The phone rang, "Hi Babes, I was just going to phone you. What, eh yeah, I'll come over right now. Give me twenty minutes. Are you ok, ok see you soon. I love you. Babes", Hester had hung up. She wants to see me ! It was me that wanted to see her, she sounded pretty serious. Shit man what's going on.

Ignition on, first gear, off we go. My hands are sweaty. Drive to Hester's in dream. Buzz buzz. "Hello" said the robotic voice at the end of the intercom. "Hi babes". Climbing the stairs, my legs feel heavy, like lead weights. Round and round I go doing a reverse direction helter skelter. Hand on door handle, door opens, the cold atmosphere hits him in the face like a sledgehammer. Feeling of woe over-powers him. He drags his heels into the living room. Hester is sitting on the couch smoking. He can see that she has been crying. She looks terrible, tired & pale but yet gorgeous at the same time. She always looks gorgeous. Socks gives her a gentle kiss on the lips. "Coffee babes" he asks. "No thanks, just get yourself one" she replies. He walks into the kitchen dragging his lead legs behind him. The feeling of impending doom weighs him down. He makes a coffee and returns to the icy cold room brrrrrr. "Socks, I have been thinking, you have got no intention of giving up the stripping even though you know how miserable it makes me", "oooh oooh" thought Socks. "Therefore you leave me no choice but to", "Hester, will you marry me". "What" gasped Hester. Socks put his coffee on the coffee table, which is a good place to put it. Do you get tea tables ? It sounds silly saying that I put my cup of tea down on the coffee table. I know that you get tea trays, as in sitting with your dinner or your lunch on a tea try watching the tv. I know that some people call them tv trays. I think that maybe that is an American thing. Certainly in Britain they are referred to as tea trays. He went down on one knee in front of Hester on the couch and said "Hester I love you with all my heart & want to live with you for the rest of my life & grow old & be buried beside you. Will you marry me". Hester just stared at him. "I was just about to dump you" she said. "I know you were" he replied. "Did you just ask me to marry you because you thought that I was going to dump you", she asked. "I admit that did hurry up the question some what but I do love you and I was going to ask you very soon". "I don't know what to say" said Hester. "Well say something because this is killing me" replied Socks. Hester just sat for a minute & stared blankly at the far wall. Socks heart was beating nine to the dozen. I don't understand that saying, nine to the dozen, why not eight or ten to the dozen. Who makes up these sayings anyway. Do people just sit about thinking things like that up. How do they catch on in the first place. I know that many moons ago in Paris when up and coming painters were skint, they would sit in cafe's all day because they couldn't afford to pay for the heating in their apartments. Apartments I like that word, it sounds much more romantic than flat or house, apartments, there I said it again, Mmmmm. So they would sit in said cafe's all day and nurse a couple of coffees. They would discuss social issues & world events & physcology. Maybe they were the ones that came up with "my heart was beating nine to the dozen". Who knows.

"Socks can you go upstairs to my bedroom please" asked Hester. "Is that a yes then darling" laughed Socks relieved. "No it isn't a yes" Socks face dropped. "It's a maybe". "What do you mean" asked Socky boy. "I mean that I am going to phone Deirdrie and ask her advice on the matter", "your what" gasped Socks. "What's it got to do with her", "I just need an independent opinion is all" exlaimed Hester. "For f**ks sake Hester would you not rather I just left and you could think about it & then phone me or something" answered Socks in dismay. "No way, I want to see you face & your reaction when I tell you the answer to your face, so on you go beat it and get upstairs". Socks just looked bewildered. He went to climb the stairs. The front door went, Socks answered it. "Do you want your newspapers delivered Mister" asked a small boy. "No" replied Socks & slammed the door in the wee boys unsupecting face. He then went upstairs as directed and into Hesters bedroom. F**k me he thought, phoning a friend, now that has got to be a first. He kicked of his shoes and lay down on the bed & stared at the ceiling. No cobwebs in Hester's ceiling. Phoning a bloody friend eh. He hadn't asked anybody's advice about asking Hester. He hadn't told anybody. Why did she need to ask somebody then. Well I suppose she was going to dump me, suppose that does make things a tad different. So she's phoning Deirdrie. Socks was back on his feet & striding up and down. What was that noise, laughter. Why was she laughing. What was there to laugh about, this is serious business man. How does Deirdrie think of me, I think she likes me pretty well. Yeah that was an ok choice choosing her, either her or Linda. She could have chosen a lot worse than Deirdrie. Saying that how do I know that she isn't phoning various people. I don't basically. There's the upstairs phone lying there, I could listen in. No she would hear the click when I pick it up. No can't do it, that would be real bad for the outcome. Shit man, what are they saying. Back lying on the bed again, back up pacing again, bed, pace, bed, pacing. Aaaah what are they saying. What if Deirdrie is telling her to say no. Would she listen to just one person. Damn this is nuts. I must be the first guy in history that this has happened to. Saying that it must have been the opposite for Henry the eight's wifes. "Just go to the tower dear, I need to send a rider with much hast with confidential royal sealed letter to Cardinal Forthingham". Shit man it's been nearly three quarters of an hour, where is she phoning, Australia.

"Socrates, come back down" Hester shouted up to old shaking like a leaf Socky boy. Socks headed slowly down the stairs, he couldn't breath, he could hardly focus on the next step. His feet made big booming sounds on ever single step, BOOM BOOM BOOM. He entered the living room. Hester was sitting on the couch still, her face was expressionless. "Do you want a refill Socks", "eh, no I don't want a bloody refill, Hesterrrrrrrr", "what" said Hester. "C'mon don't" splutterted out Socks. "Oh do you want to know my answer to your question" asked the minx. "Eh well yeah, that would be nice, sometime today please". "Take a seat then, no not over there, beside me dafty". Socks sat beside her. "Socrates look into my eyes", Socks looked into her eyes. "Socrates the answer is yes". "We're getting married in the morning, ding dong the bells are going to chime" sang Socks laughing. "Come here you" Socks shouted & grabbed Hester & cuddled her for the UK. Hester held him tight to her & closed her eyes. They held onto each other for what must have been nearly ten minuters. Then Socks pulled away "Hester I am giving up the stripping babes", "no your not Socks" replied Hester. "What do you mean I'm not, I thought", "Socks I want a big wedding, a big reception, loads of people, so that requires money, you are going to strip your wee ass of to help pay for it". Socks gave her a big beaming smile. "I love you so much babes". "Then after we get married I might just want another baby, so you will continue stripping to pay for that expense as well. In fact I will be giving you a hard time if you don't have gigs". Socks smile spreaded to both of his lugs. "I thought you didn't want anymore kids", "I didn't but I have been getting a bit broody recently & I think I might have changed my mind on that one". Socks grabbed her and gave her another Socky boy special cuddle. "Just one thing though Mr Socrates, I want you to come straight home to me after every gig, no hanging about chatting up these tarts, gig finishes, you pack up your shit & get home here, bringing in a Chinese carry out on the way ok", "ok wife" laughed Socks.

"So will we have an engagement party then babes" Socks asked Hester. "Not really bothered about that honey, I more interested in the big day, we will have to get planning". What does she mean have to get planning thought Socks. I was planning on being engaged for at least a couple of years & she's talking about planning already. I've just bloody popped the question. "Oh Socks just one thing darling, one very important thing, no more full monty. I am the only one that is going to get to see your dick from now on, that's what makes me special, nobody else gets to see it apart from me. Are you ok with that because it is not up for debate", "Yeah babes no worries, i'm sick of the tying up process anyway, it's defo not good for you". "Promise me Socrates, I am deadly serious about this, if I find out that you are still doing it from somebody then it's all over ok". "Hester I promise you that I will not do the full monty anymore". "Ok honey" said Hester "I love you". She gave Socks a big smacker on the lips and walked out of the room. Socks stared after her for a while, then sat down on the couch & held his head in his hands.

Eighteen

Dog had just watched the movie Midnight Express & his mind was working overtime. He had seen the movie on various occasions over the years but this time it had a major impact on him. Maybe it was the way he was feeling at the time, maybe it was just a coincidence but whatever it was the cogwheels in Dog's brain were turning.

For anybody that has not seen Midnight Express, it is a true story about a young American guy called Willian (Billy) Hayes. He was done for possession of cannabis in Turkey and sentenced to fours years. He endured physical and mental cruelty but remained optimistic about his release mainly due to his family's persistance. Due to political unrest at the time in Istanbul in the early 1970's with suicide bombers and tensions at there highest between the East and the West the prosecution had the case re-opened and Billy's charge was made up to pushing drugs rather than possession. He was given a life sentence of thirty years. In 1975 after nearly been driven insane Billy's family planned his escape and in 1975 he did just that crossing the borders into Greece and then back to the States three weeks later.

Now what is it about this you may well ask that got Dog's interest levels soaring in the clouds. Well I will get to that shortly. William Hayes years after his escape wrote his story. His story got published and maverick film director Alan Parker decided that he was going to take it onboard as a project. Alan directed amazing movies, they have all stood the test of time, Mississippi Burning, Angel Heart & The Commitments all had two major aspects in common. They were visually superb & had legendary soundtracks. Midnight Express was no exception. It was visually stunning combining the Istanbul hustle and bustle with the solitude of the hell hole prison. The music was by Giorgio Moroder, think Tangerine dream mixed with Kraftwerk and you will come close to the electronic soundtrack. The use of thumping heartbeats at the start of the movie during the drugs smuggling scene & the escape scene at the end propel the viewer into the heart of the movie and you can feel the tension in your toes.

Dog's phone rang, it was Brutus. "Dog what's this pish about vans and production sets & ambient music man", "it's not pish you reprobate, listen I'll explain, I have phoned everybody and left a message, are you free on Tuesday night, I need a meet". Tuesday night arrived and the guys plus Trish were all seated in the bar of the Marriott Hotel in Glasgow's Anderson area. "Well" said Trish, "what is this all about Dog"."Guys did you all see that documentary the other week about the Welsh male strippers, The Centaurs" said Dog. Everybody nodded and grunted. They had all either watched it at the time or taped it and watched it later. What the Centaurs done was to take a van to every gig with various production set pieces, whether it was a bed or a coat stand or a makeshift shower. "Well" said Dog, "I think it is time for us to take the show to the next level, we need to do the same, but in doing that, we need a brand new show, new routines, new music, not just any old music, but great music, a soundtrack to the show. We already have signature tunes, they can stay but we need more. We already have the image with the kilts, but we need to expand on that".

Everybody was looking at each other and muttering and grunting. "I don't know" said Trish, "that sounds like a lot of hard work & extra expense Dog, The cost of a van, the cost of the set pieces, more choreography, it's all time and money". "So" replied Dog, "So what Trish, don't you want the Highlanders to be one of the best acts on your books, a good show, the NEW Highlander show needs that time and money. There are younger, good looking guys coming out of the woodwork all the time, they can see the we are not getting any younger, these guys are nipping at our heals Trish, we need a new fresh show and we need it now". "Hey man you have been hanging about Socks too much" said Levi, "shut it you ya fud" replied Socks. "What do you all think" asked Dog. "I think you need your head looked at" said Dave. "Any constructive comments" said Dog beginning to look annoyed. "Well mate, I think it is a good idea and I do think the show would benefit but you need to look at the bigger picture" commented Hero. "Yeah big picture thinking" injected Gloves. Everybody just looked at Gloves and ignored him. "What do you mean dude" asked Dog. "What I mean is that you have to look at the number of big gigs we do that would make this move constructive" said Hero. "I mean big gigs like social clubs, nightclubs, hotels and bingo halls because there would be no point with small gigs like pubs like and restaurants". "Why not" replied Dog. "Why not, because the set pieces would take up half of the dancefloor, that's if there was a dancefloor in the first place". "Not necessarily the case" replied Dog getting huffy, "for instance if we were doing a pub gig and Socks was doing his business man suited and booted routine, a coat-stand would look". "Oh right" said Levi, "yeah that makes a lot of sense lets take a big van to the gig for one coatstand". "I don't just mean one coat-stand, each performer could have one smaller set piece" argued Dog. "I'll give you a smaller set piece, a boot size ten, right up your arse" laughed Dave. "Dog I just don't think there is enough big gigs anymore to warrant the purchase of a van" said Trish, "I appreciate what you are saying and I think it is good that you are thinking about the show and trying to improve it but I just don't think it is financially viable". Dog just stared at the floor the wind totally taken out of his sails. "She's right mate" Socks offered up, "it is changed days, it is not like the old days where we would be doing a big social club every Friday night & a bingo hall or nightclub on a Saturday. These days people just don't want to spend the money on full shows all the time".

Dog new that Trish & Socks had a point. They were doing a lot more one and two man gigs. This year they seemed to have done half of the number of full shows as last year. It was all pubs these days, sometimes social clubs, but it was for strip-o-grams, in and out. It wasn't just the stripping it was all over. Bands were going out in two's rather than four's or five's. Rather than a solo singer getting booked for a two hour spot it was a one hour spot split into two thiry minute sketches. Then there would be karaoke or a dj playing during the break. Comedians were doubling up with hen and stag nights. It all seemed to be down to value of money to the punter and that was deemed to be more for less. He knew this before he called the meeting. It was part of the reason, he thought that something had to be done, but apathy had also set in and dug in the claws. People didn't want to take the risk to speculate to accumulate. He decided there and then that he would make differences in his own way. New costumes, new music, new routines. Harder workouts, get that body in better shape. Take better care of himself, more early nights, healthier eating.

Everbody made their excuses and left. Dog was last to go. He sat thinking about the way it used to be. They never used to take their own cars, it was everybody in two cars or one if it was a family sized car and they could all squeeze in. It was more of an event. A Highlander full show, something to really live for, a reason. The build up by the dj to the crowd. The atmosphere, the smell of the venue. Then afterwards, The China Sea in Gordon St in the city centre. Great Chinese food good company. The Tunnel nightclub in Mitchell lane, a piece of history for the Highlanders. Racing back from a gig in Dundee or Perth to beat that two am curfew.The purpose seemed to have been lost. Now it was just routine. Dog hated routine.

The cold truth was that being a male stripper just wasn't as good as it used to be. It wasn't just Dog that felt that way, all the guys felt it to varying degrees. Outside factors, marriage, kids, jobs, financial pressures all weighed down on the guys the same as it does anybody else. The Highlanders weren't young guys anymore. When most of them started they didn't have much in the way of responsibilities but that all seemed a distant memory now. Don't get me wrong you went through peaks & troughs, high's & low's. Some weeks you were right up for it, some weeks you weren't. It had definitely became more of a JOB. One thing was for sure was that the money was still a major motivation. Most people were out spending at the weekends, when you are in the entertaiment game you work at the weekend, so you are usually having a good time and getting paid for it.

You defo had to have thick skin in this line of business. "Your not the stripper are you", "my man's got a better body than you", "my man's got a bigger dick than you", "don't give up your day job", "don't you think your getting a bit old for this carry on". That's the down side but for every cloud there is a silver lining, "you were amazing, awesome", "your some dancer, what a mover", "oh my god your yummy", "you have some body, I love your pecs". So yip you could be down one minute & up the next. Then there was the bitching about strippers you were working with, "that guy with the Elvis haircut is crap, he should get a haircut for starters and then some of the women might actually like him". You can be sure though that if some woman is bitching to you that Elvis is crap then somebody else is bitching to Elvis that you are crap also. So it's swing's & roundabouts.

We used to always look forward to gigs. If you were working during the day for instance, it was the thought of the gig in the evening that would sustain you. It was like a social occasion. More often than not though if you are working through the day now, then when you get in from your shift the last thing you feel like doing is getting your gear ready, getting the old g-strings ironed for a hard night ahead, shaving (chest as well as face), showering, feeding, pruning. You just want to come in from work and relax and crash out, but you can't. Once you got going though you were usually fine, you would get a second wind and just get on with it. You would be in the car and heading to your boabey oot destination and it would be yeeehah lets do this. The buzz would return with a vengeance. What is really crap though was that you used to always walk into a gig and through the crowd & they would go mental, screaming and hollering. Now well you get that now and again, but more often than not it is just indifference. "Oh is that the stripper". Smashing eh. Oh the old days, I miss the old days.

Nineteen

Blue eyed boy vs the blame hound

One thing about Dog, for a good few years he was the blue eyed boy. It went back to Mark's day when he had the stint of manager & continued onto into Trish's reign. It was sporadic though, he would fade into oblivion from time to time. Yip it had to be said he walked on water most of the time though, couldn't put a foot wrong. So he got most of the one man jobs & nearly all of the two man jobs along with a mish mash of whomever else was available. Back then you would normally give your back teeth to be the other guy because we all wanted the work.

So it was then that the blame hound was founded. Yeah and that would be old Socky boy. You see we more or less relied on Mark & to a lesser extent Trish at the start of her managerial role to provide the work. You would wait on the phone ringing informing you of who was working where. They would be the only source of the work. Then as we saw the likes of Dog the "blue eyed boy" getting more and more work we decided to wisen up. Socks became the main contact for a number of years with the agents. Whenever an agent didn't want to go through Trish direct for one or two man gigs they would phone Socks and he would divide the work up fairly or fairlyish between the guys. Then the odd agent would want a full show on the quiet, this would happen now and again but was difficult as Trish would more or less find out through the grapevine that we had appeared here or there. What would usually work was if the show was on a mid-week night or a Sunday, then it was a goer.

What would happen though is Socks would bring in jobs & inform the guys and then Trish would bring in full shows that clashed with the dates & then it all went pear shaped. Socks would have to run around bringing in freelance strippers to cover the incognito jobs and then the venues wouldn't be happy because they weren't getting one of the Highlanders as promised. So it got fairly messy from time to time. Socks would have to put his hands in the air from time to time and that is how the blame hound title got handed to him. It was quite funny for a while he was always getting caught out. Then he didn't have the time to deal with the agents & the mantle got handed over to Hero. The swine never seemed to get as caught as often as Socks though so to this day Socrates is still the blame hound. Nowadays though Trish gets to know about ninety-five percent of the outside work, it just grew into too much of a monster to control.

Tying up - a users guide

I have touched before on the pastime called "tying up". Male strippers the world over will be familiar with this phrase. I will go into some detail here of what is involved in said process. If one wants one's penis to appear bigger onstage then one shall have to go through this routine :

(1) Take some pornographic material, usually a magazine
(2) Take a pair of sharp scissors, the small jewel models are best
(3) Take either a standard elasticated band of reasonable thickness (nb. this is very important, if the band is too thin there could be a major circulation problem) or a length of trouser elastic
(4) Find a private place. Usually a toilet cubicle or large cupboard or cellar are obvious choices.
(5) Open pornographic material and starting stroking the penis in a backward and forward motion until stimulation is achieved
(6) Once penis is in a semified state take elasticated band and wrap around the meat and two veg at least twice so that the elastic is tight & the blood remains in the penis.
(7) Finish putting on costume of choice
(8) Pray that the DJ doesn't f**k about with some obscure remix of the Bee Gee's while you are striding up and down with an elasticated band around your cock
(9) Start getting really pissed of as the dj still hasn't announced you yet
(10) Your still not onstage and you are now unable to feel your willie
(11) At last you get announced onstage
(12) You are onstage jumping about like a fanny (as usual)
(13) You come offstage and find private place & use said scissors to VERY CAREFULLY remove the elasticated band
(14) You scream with pain at the release of the elastic, this is a combination of real pain and a psychological moment as you know it's going to hurt
(15) You give you balls and base of your stem a good massage to get some feeling back in
(16) Finally you wonder (for the thousandth time) what long-term damage you are actually doing

Socks probably wondered a bit more than the other guys because things hadn't felt quite right down there for a while now. Yeah things were a bit out of order, the plumbing was defo not the way it should be. For a start there was more frequent visits to the john, a lot of starting and stopping on the streamie front. Yip there was no doubt about it Socrates was peeing like an old man. Then there was that uncomfortable feeling also, a kind of knotted feeling at the base of his stem. No bloody wonder considering the abuse it had been receiving for years.

"Hey Hero how are you doing my old son" Socks asked. "Not five bad matee, hows tricks with you" Hero replied."Tricks are ok bud but I am not at all happy about my meat & and two veg at the mo", "really, that doesn't sound too good old chap, pray tell why not" sniggered Hero. "Why do you bloody think, eh might it possibly be the fact that I have been wrapping a rope around them for the last eight years might have a slight impact on the situation" answered Socks with more than a hint of sarcasm. "Well now you come to mention it my groin has definitely seen better days as well" replied Hero. "What's your symptoms" asked Dr Socrates, "well doctor I would say prolonged orgasm"," f**k off you" laughed Socks, "I am serious ya big shite", "ok sorry, well it defo feels a bit on the sensitive side from time to time & I am pissing more" said Hero. "Yeah man me too and sometimes I feel like Mike Tyson has given my balls a good going over like he has been practicing his speed ball skills", "hahaha what you like" laughed Hero. "Listen mate don't tell the guys but I have made an appointment at the Royal to get them checked out, I need peace of mind that I have not done any permanent damage", "what, really, your yanking my chain" laughed Hero but thinking to himself that it was a really smart move on old Socky's front and maybe he should do likewise. "Mate promise me that you will not tell the guys" said Socks seriously. "Mate I promise" replied Hero.

Hester was the one that was responsible for the hospital appointment. She had been nagging Socks for a couple of months to do something about it. He had eventually folded and went to his doctor. He had not mentioned anything about stripping or tying up of course. Just said that the plumbing wasn't right. The Doc had set up an appointment at the hospital & his card came through the door, he was due to go a week on Wednesday at 10am. "Awright matee how the hell are you" Levi asked Socks. "Brand new my old cocker spaniel, how's yourself" replied Socks, " much better than you mate, I've not got a plumbing problem downstairs" laughed Levi. "I'll f**king kill him" shouted Socks down the phone to Levi and hung up. "Right fanny baws, I thought you promised me not to tell anybody ya wank", Socks screamed down the phone at Hero. "I don't remember that" laughed Hero. "Well is that right, you can tell your mum that is the last time I am sleeping with her" said Socks, "she wouldn't have you mate" laughed Hero not getting riled by Socks dig "she's got taste".

The Wednesday in question came much to soon like a male virgin with his first shag. Socks had to fast from midnight the night before and was only allowed sips of water. He was nervous, infact he was extremely nervous. He had received a handout from the hospital that explained the procedure. The patient was given a general antiseptic and then when he was out cold a flexible plastic THIN cord with a tiny camera on the end was inserted into the patients jap's eye and shoved all the way up his penis (aaaaaahhhhhhhhh !!!) into his bladder (aaaaaaahhhhhh !!). Socks hands were clammy, he thought he could handle anything after doing a full highlander show in front of one thousand five hundred screaming she devils in the Mecca bingo hall in Easterhouse, but he was wrong, he was shiting bricks.

"Babes don't worry, you will be fine" said Hester reassuringly. She was trying to offer Socks some empathy but she didn't have a cock and didn't know how it felt. She didn't know that if you were a guy, any guy watching a film or tv programme and some dude gets a flying kick into the goolies then you automatically grab you nuts & close your legs tight as if you were the poor bastard receiving the volley. She was only trying to help, but wasn't. "Hester you've not got a cock" said Socks. "Well I am sure that you are glad that I don't have a cock Socks" replied Hester. Socks just made a face, he wasn't in a joking mood. Hester drove him to the hospital and dropped him off. "I'll be back with Connor at five-ish, ok babes", "yeah ok" answered Socks looking dismal. "You will be fine honey, don't worry" and she drove off.

"Ok" thought Socks, ward 5, third floor. He took the elevator, one, hands getting sweaty again, two, beads of sweat appearing on his brow, three, lower back area starts feeling quite moist. Doors open, ok lets find the ward, *elbows & toes*, no, *knees and ankles*, no, *tummies and bummies*, nope, ah here we go, *the stems ward.* He handed his card over to the receptionist and was asked to take a seat. "Where do you want me to take it" Socks asked her and received a non answer glare. Humour, yeehah, his humor had returned. Why though, why was he using humour at a time like this. Aaah he knew, coping mechanism. He was using humour to cope with his situation, that was good wasn't it. At least he was trying, "very trying" thought the receptionist to herself. "Mr Socrates" a young blonde good looking nurse called entering the waiting area. "That's moi" said Socks. "Follow me please Mr Socrates" said Fiona. He knew she was called Fiona because her name plate said so. "Ok Fiona lead the way" said Socks, she smiled at him and walked on. Hold on, what was he doing, what was he thinking. She was probably going to see his wee willie and he was giving her the patter. Jesus she would laugh her head off. The wee chap would probably just shrivel up and go and hide inside his body, it would become a vagina, a flower. Socks would become a bird with male breasts. "Doctor there seems to have been a clerical error, Mr Socrates has got a vagina not a penis". He started sweating again. They arrived at an area in the ward with six beds in two rows of three with two big white dividers shutting them of from the rest of the ward. There was two guys there already wearing gowns and sitting up on the their beds, one was white one was black.

"Mr Socrates please get undressed and put on the gown that is in your wardrobe, there is also a dressing gown if you are feeling cold & slippers, the Doctor will be around to speak to you shortly", "ok thanks Fiona will do" said Socks. Fiona hussled off. Socks turned to the two guys "awright guys how ya doing", they both muttered a reply. Socks started getting undressed, when he was removing his jeans one of the guys pipped up "mate your meant to close the curtain around you when you are getting undressed", "oh yeah right, sorry" replied Socks and closed the curtain. He laughed to himself, always in stripping mode, can't help himself, even in a hospital in front of two guys, haha. He finished getting undressed put on the gown, didn't bother with the dressing robe as he was still feeling a bit hot and bothered but put on the slippers and opened the curtain and sat up on the bed.

"Do you think Socks is getting his baws felt yet" Hero said on the phone to Brutus, "Yeah well, he probably is, I bet the big poof is enjoying it as well","haha" laughed Hero, "yeah he is probably lying there going left a bit, right a bit, that's the spot right there hahaha". Truth was though that they were both dying to here the outcome of Socks visit to the Royal. Socks proactiveness with this sketch made the rest of the Highlanders aware of their own probs with their gonnads.

Socks glanced at the two dudes and they looked even

more worried than him, one was about twenty five (the black dude) with a crew cut and was well made, tall, about 210lbs with a well trimmed goatey. He was thumbing through some magazine on mens health, "too late" thought Socks. The other dude was slightly older late twenties & had a blonde pony tail, skinny and tall and looked like a hippy. He was just sitting staring out the window. Socks didn't think there had been any chat between the two guys. "You guys in to get your stems checked out" asked Socks as if it was the most natural question in the world. The two guys looked at each other and the hippy dude said "yeah man, sure am, what about you", "yip" said Socks and turned to the black guy. "Yes actually I am here for an investigation on my penis", "ooohh investigation of my penis" Socks thought to himself, this guy was very polite. He continued "my girlfriend made the appointment with my doctor because I refused to, it was then that I realised that I had to address the problem and confront it face to face", "eh yeah, right" said Socks, "eh me too more or less, my fiancé moaned at me for ages before I done anything about it", "same for me dudes" said the hippy guy, "the love of my life", "eh" thought Socks, "well she just pure kept on my case like man, you know man, it was like a big burden man, my small shoulders couldn't take the strain dudes", "this guys on drugs" thought Socks. The black guy struck up "guys I feel the empathy in this room, it's like a fellow suffering bond, it's like a subject that you feel you can't approach with your colleagues and friends", "especially my bloody friends" thought Socks. "I couldn't have put it better myself dude" said the hippy guy.At that point Fiona re-appeared with another two guys and gave them the same instructions. They muttered their greetings to the other guys and closed their curtains to get undressed, unlike Socks. When the curtains re-opened they fell into the same line of conversation as the other guys. They were both a bit older than the others, say early forties. One guy was bald but with a muscular physique and the other guy had a mad bush of dark hair, big eyebrows that met in the middle giving him a mad scientist look and was a fair bit overweight. Both were quite short in height. About an hour passed and still nobody came to see them. The last patient didn't appear either that's if there was a last patient. There was six beds but only five guys. "Maybe there was only met to be five guys" said one of the new blokes, "nah" said Socks "bet he shat out of it, I was nearly not going to come either". The others all nodded their heads in agreement. Turned out that they had all been given different arrival times and that they were all fifteen minutes apart. Didn't make the slightest bit of a difference as still no Doctor had appeared and it was 11.45.

Twenty

"Do you think Socks is splayed out on a table with his legs wrenched apart and some dude wearing marigolds feeling his baws" Dog asked Dave on the phone. "Don't know what your laughing about your next" sniggered Dave evilly. "Get it right up you Dave" scowled Dog on the other end of the phone. "Well at least I've not got to bother, I don't wrap an elastic band around my cock every weekend" Dave continued to laugh. "You don't wrap an elastic band around your cock because you've not got a cock you've got maggot" sniggered Dog. "Yeah yeah, you laugh, I'll have the last one though when I'm an old man and don't have to have a nurse maid twenty four hours a day", "the nurse maid wouldn't have you ya ugly bastard" laughed Dog.

When they both finished slagging each other and hung up, Dave sat back and thought about Socks. He hoped he was alright, they had grown pretty tight over the years & considered Socks a close friend. It was all ok having a laugh but it might be something more serious than they were all laughing about. Yeah, Dave hoped that Socks was ok.

The Doctor appeared just after mid-day & muttered his apologies to everybody, something to do with a short staffed problem. "As long as the dude with the tiny camera turned up", Socks thought. The Doctor pulled the curtain around the hippy guy who musty have been first to arrive and they could all hear the Doctors lowered voice & then onto the black guy next and then Socks. He pulled the curtain around Socks bed. "Mr Socrates" the Doctor said checking his list. That's correct said Socks. "Once again let me apologise for the delay" said the doctor, "no worries" replied Socks. "Ok what will happen is that in about fifteen minutes an orderly will appear and will push your bed down to theatre, when you arrive a nurse will check your personal details, name, address, dob etc. You will then be wheeled into surgery and a Doctor will explain the process of what will happen next, are you ok with these instructions Mr Socrates", "yes no worries Doc" replied Socks. The doctor moved on to the next bed. An orderly appeared two minutes after the Doc had spoke to Socks. He wheeled away the hippy dude who was looking pretty mournful. They all waved goodbye to him as if he was a long lost friend and would never be seen again. One by one a different orderly appeared for them all and they were all wheeled away.

Socks was lying in his scratcher outside the theatre and an older nurse called Mary was taking his details. None of the other guys were there, where were they, had they already been taken in. He lay there for what seemed like an age but it was only ten minutes. This was the worse part, the waiting. "For Christ sake Socrates man up, man right up, your no pussy, your not going into battle" his positive (+) side told him, "yes you are man, you are going into battle, your penis is going to have to fight for it's life, it will be man handled and thrown about and you will be out cold and not be able to defend yourself" his negative (-) side told himself. "shut up you don't listen to that pussy" said (+), "who the hell are you calling a pussy ya pyscho" said (-). "You, I'm calling you a pussy, that's right always trying to talk him out of things when he just needs to be a man" answered (+), "a man eh, a man is it eh" replied (-), "yeah a man, c'mon Socks me old son man up, come on now man up" said (+).

"Oh shut up you two, you are always going on, why can't you just get on, why can't we all just live together" thought Socks. At this point in the proceedings the hippy guy was wheeled out a door to the left of where Socks was lying and wheeled up beside him. Socks strained over the side of his bed to get a better look, he was out cold. He looked relatively peaceful, no visible slobbers at the side of his mouth or anything. Then the nurse who had taken his details re-appeared and wheeled him into a room on the right. She informed him that the Doctor would be with him shortly and then he was alone again. It was a small room with two shuttered swinging doors at the far end. There was a worksurface on either side of Socks with various medical accouterments adorning it. The light in the room was very strong, Socks blinked his eyes and closed them to ease the uncomfortable glare. When he opened them again there was two guys staring down at him. They were both wearing green gowns and these mini beanie cap things you see on ER and Casualty that look like somebody has stretched a Joseph and his amazing Technicolor condom over their nappers. They were both older, say late forties. "Hello Mr Socrates, I am Dr Smythe and my colleague is Dr Farquar". Dr Farquar was smiling down at him. "I thought that Farquar was a forename not a surname" said Socks. "That is a common mistake" answered Dr Farquar. Dr Smythe continued "ok Mr Socrates I am going to give you an injection which will put you to sleep and then we shall insert a thin plastic cord with a tiny but very powerful camera on the end into your jap's eye and up your penis into your bladder". "How powerful is the camera" enquired Socks, "eh I believe it is a 3.2 mega pixel camera" said Dr Smythe, "why do you want to know", "just interested" replied Socks. "Eh ok Mr Socrates you will not feel a thing as you are out cold. Dr Farquar will now administer the injection". "Mr Socrates" said Dr Farquar "when I administer the injection I will ask you to count to ten, by ten at the latest you will be asleep".

"How do you think Socks is getting on" Trish asked Brutus. "Probably left leg first as usual" replied Brutus. "Pardon" said Trish. "He'll be fine Trish, don't worry, Socks is a tough dude", "are you sure Brutus, he seemed quite worked up about it", "yeah don't worry Trish seriously this is a walk in the park to Socks".

"Eh Dr Farquar I'm not sure that I want to go through with this, I am suddenly feeling a lot better" Socks bleated. "Mr Socrates there is really nothing to worry about, you will be fine" said Dr Farquar. "I don't know, I want children you know at some stage, well not now or anything but in the near future maybe" Socks bleated a bit further. "C'mon now Mr Socrates, are you a man or a mouse" interrupted Dr Smythe."Mouse" answered Socks looking bashful. Dr Farquar started administering the injection. Start counting to ten please Mr Socrates. "one, two, three, four, five, sixxxxxx". Socks was out cold.

Raindrops keep falling on my head, di di do do di di do do. Socks opened his eyes. "Aaah bright, too bright". Socks closed his eyes.

Keep falling on my head, di di do do di di do do. Socks opened his eyes "why were all these people standing over him & why were they all smiling". He was in the recovery area, where he had originally been and where the hippy dude was brought back to. The people that looked down at him were Farquar and Smythe, the older nurse that pushed him in, another couple of nurses and a female Doctor with the same green gown as the other docs but with no condom on her head. Infact the other Docs had removed their condoms as well, I hope they threw them out, you were only meant to use them once.

"Awright my big darling, how are you feeling gorgeous" said the female Doctor. "F**k you" thought Socks, "eh never better thanks, hows yourself". Socks was brought up to be polite. "Well big boy that's it all over, the orderly will take you back to the ward in a couple of minutes where you can have a small light lunch and just rest until a Doctor appears later to give you the outcome from the investigation". "Thank you Miss Marple" thought Socks. "Thank you Doctor" said Socks being courteous. "Why were they all still smiling like that and what did she mean big boy and what's with the patter darling, gorgeous etc, that's hardly professional Doctor lingo, that's my lingo" thought Socks. The crowd dispersed and Socks was left to his thoughts. "Big boy eh they must give you a wank so that your cock is bigger when they shove that cable up it" said (-), "no no, there will be some drug in the injection that will give you a semi, like viagra or something" replied (+), "what you wish. both Smythe and Farquar would be taking turns each ripping the head of it" answered (-), "don't listen to him Socratres it will all be above board an professional, even if there is an element of truth in what he is saying then it would probably be the female doc doing the wanking" said (+), "aye right Farquar and Smythe" replied (-), "no no, the female doc" said (+).

"Awright pal" said the orderly. "I'll just take you back to the ward". "Hey Bro, do you know why that lot were all grinning at me like Cheshire cats" asked Socks. "Yeah mate, when you were out cold you were babbling on about this and that seemingly, but you kept saying to Dr Tommlinson, your getting it, your getting it doll", "no way" laughed Socks, "was that the female doc", "sure was pal" said the orderly. No wonder they were all laughing.

Back at the ward the hippy guy and the black dude were sitting up munching into sandwiches. "Awright guys" Socks asked, "yeah mate, you" answered the hippy. "Yeah ok thanks". He sat up in bed once the orderly wheeled him back into place and inspected his weener. It looked a bit battered and bruised. There was a ball of cotton wool taped onto the end of his dick and it had a little blood on it. The nurse came to see him and asked him what he wanted for lunch. He opted for the tuna mayo wholemeal sandwich and a orange juice. She asked to see his willie which he thought was a bit unsual, she looked at it and said fine it looks ok. Socks was nearly embarrassed and it takes a lot to embarrass Socrates. He wondered how many dicks she saw in a month, probably plenty. "Just to let you know that the first couple of times you go for a pee it will be midly uncomfortable" the nurse informed him. "No worries Fiona" answered Socks.

He ate his sandwich and drunk his orange juice. He still felt sleepy and nodded of for about forty minutes. When he awoke the initial Doctor that had been so apologetic was with the hippy dude. Bye the time he got to Socks the orderly had wheeled the guy with the big eyebrows back into his slot. The Doc pulled the curtains around old Socky boy and took a seat by the bed. "Mr Socrates I am pleased to inform you that the investigation found no problem with your bladder, you have the all clear", "that's great news thanks Doc" replied Socks. "Do you have any idea yourself why you might have encountered this discomfort, have you had an injury or anything" the Doc enquired. "No idea Doc" Socks lied. "Well it's all good anyway, you can go home in an hour or so once you feel up for it, is anybody coming to collect you", "yes thanks Doc, my fiancé is getting me", "ok then the only other thing was did the nurse mention to you about the discomfort peeing", "yes she did thanks doc, no worries". The Doc moved on to the next patient.

Socks looked at his watch 3.45pm, Hester was getting him in at 5ish. He wondered whether to ask the other dudes how they got on but decided that it was too personal. The hippy and the black guy seemed happy enough looking but still decided not to say anything. They just chatted about general stuff and a canteen lady came around and gave them some tea, they weren't allowed coffee, to high in caffeine. At 4.30 Socks decided to go for a pee. The nurse Fiona came up and asked where he was going. She told him to leave the door slightly ajar and that she would be outside if he needed her. "Eh, what did she mean needed her, for what, I can shake my own John Thomas thank you very much". Ok in the toilet, remove the tape and the cotton wool, nae bother, ok let's do it, legs apart over the toilet bowl, weener pointed in the downward trajectory, pee, aaaaaaahhhhhhh, f**kkkkkkkkkkkkkkkkk, mutherf*kerrrrrrrrrrrrrrrrrrrrrr, f**kkkkkkk. Oh no no stop stop, what the f**k, mild discomfort ma ass". "Mr Socrates are you ok in there" shouted nurse Fiona. "Am I f**k" shouted back Socks, "I thought you said mild discomfort". He had to get this pee out, ok here goes again , pee, aaaaaaaaaahhhhhh, jobbbbbbbiiiiiiieeeeesssss, mutherf**kerrrrrrr,aaaaaaaaaaaaahh. Well this went on for about fifteen minutes until all the urine was out. He staggered back to bed and collapsed on top of it. "You ok mate" asked the hippy, "yeah fine man" answered Socks. "You been to the toilet yet dudes" he asked the other guys and they both shook their heads. "Good luck" he said and they both looked at each other baffled.

At five bells a senior nurse appeared to inform Socks that his fiancé had arrived to take him home. He got dressed and was escorted by the senior nurse into a small waiting room at the end of the ward. Hester and Connor both gave him a warm welcome. The senior nurse Marjory came back in to sign him out and to take his wrist band off. She quickly ran through the Doctors findings again and that there was nothing to worry about. She was actually a total gem as she asked Socks if he worked out & Socks informed her that he regularly visited the gym. She informed him that for some reason athletes seemed to suffer from this complaint especially long distance runners. Something to do with movement and the bladder getting pushed against the stomach. Socks started to wonder if using the weightlifting belt had anything to do with it. Anything but tying a bit of elasticated band around his boabey.

When they got home Hester asked Socks if there was anything that he needed. He told her that he was fine, just not to worry if she heard lots of colourful language and shouting when he went to the toilet. She just gave him a look, he was very, very weird sometimes.

Twenty-one

A Stage show comes along once in a blue moon. When it does, it's usually the cause of much excitement. Lots of reasons, the raised stage, the high ceiling, the large floor space, the sound system, the atmosphere, the smoke, the lights & most of all the anticipation of a great memorable gig.

That was the reason that Trish had been excited for the last two months. The Highlanders had been booked for a one off gig in the Majestic Nightclub in Motherwell. She wasn't only excited though, she was stressed. There was so much to organise & worry about. There was all the PR from her side, posters, flyers, right music, getting a guy to video it, organising the guys i.e. were they all in good enough shape, had they all been training, taking sunbeds, was their outfits in good nick. Then she had to worry that the club done their side of things right. They had to get adverts in the local press, radio, they had to put her posters up, they had to get PR staff out on the town the previous weekend. She hated relying on other people, that was why nobody worked for her & she done all the agency work herself. What about Hero, would Hero be on-time. She would arrange to meet the Guys at some pre-arranged place.

The Guys all met in the cafe at Marcos Gym at Templeton business Centre in Bridgeton. The strippers all had on the same outfits. Jeans, white t-shirts, cat boots & the black & gold embroidered Highlander jackets. Hero went with Trish in her Beemer & the rest of the guys went in another two cars. They arrived together at the Majestic & they had to walk by the girls in the audience to get to the dressing room at the side of the stage. The place was rammed & the guys got a phenomenal reception when they walked through. They nodded and waved at the Girls. They felt like Take That, it was an amazing buzz. On arriving at the dressing room the nerves began to settle in, "where's my feckin mic" moaned Dave. "Last time I seen your mic cable it was hanging out of your arse son" laughed Socks. "Shut it you, or it will be hanging out of your arse shortly" growled Dave. "Ooh kinky" retorted Socks. "Hey Dave why don't you look in your mic bag" laughed Dog. "well thanks for that Dog, I wouldn't have thought of that.

The noise coming from outside the dressing room was intense, just a massive hummer of voices. The fact that it was so busy & was getting video'd was enough to make Tom Jone's dick disappear inside him. This is a good time to explain something to a very popular question as I get asked this a lot at gigs. "Hey Mr Stipper, how come when you are dancing with all these hot chicks you don't get an erection". I can answer that in one word "adrenalin". You see nerves & adrenalin shrink the wee guy, he's not happy, not playing, hibernating for the winter, in the huff. So Jennifer Lopez could be bouncing up and down on your crotch during some simulation in a routine, nothing is going to happen, nada. I hope that clears this sensitive, delicate question up ?

Trish appeared at the door. "Dave your on, Guys be ready to go onstage in fifteen minutes". "Trish is the video guy there yet" asked Levi. "Yip he's set up at the back of the venue & is ready to go". "Guys I want 110%, get ready, i'll be back in fifteen minutes", "Ok love" replied Hero. "Hoi Brutus where are you going man", said Socks, "I'm going for a pre-show shit" replied Brutus. "I need one as well man, just nip it there's no time" said Hero. "No I can't nip it" said Brutus & disappeared out the door. "That fud had better not be late" said Socks. "He's got ten minutes".

"It's been three days to the hour since you've been gone" Ruby Turners silky sweet vocals appeared over the sound system. "Classic" said Dog, "That'll be Dave on then". The sound got cranked up a couple of notches as Dave went on, "well man how was it" asked Hero, "World Classsss" replied Dog, "Aggghhh" shouted Levi, "it's a conspiracy". "Well did you inspect the knickers then" said Socks, "I certainly did" replied Dog, "well" said Socks, "the popular verdict is that they are clean" said Dog. "Where are they then" asked Socks, "they're still out there" said Dog, "what do you mean" said Socks, "I mean old Socky boy that they are still out there, as in they are not in here" replied Dog. "Why aren't they in here" asked Socks, "because fanny baws, I left them out there, as did you". "Right Brutus your last on, you bring them in" said Socks, "I'm not bringing them in" replied Brutus. "why not", "because who knows where they've been I'm not touching them" said Brutus. "Dog has just told you that they are clean", "yes but me thinks that Dog might possibly be talking shite & that's what's probably on the back part of the knickers".

Brutus's number came on and he disappeared onstage. "Did you clock these two birds hanging over the edge of the left hand stairs onto the stage" asked Levi, "Yeah the one with the leather trousers & her mate with the black dress" said Hero. "Their right up for it" said Levi. "Have they been used yet" asked Socks. Levi & Hero looked at each other, "Yeah they have", "your a couple of lying bastards, you don't know" laughed Socks. "Well I do believe that one is on first in the second half & I do believe that the bird with the leather breeks is getting used and abused" said Socks.

Brutus appeared back in the dressing room. "did you get them" asked Socks, "what" said Brutus, "the knickers" said Socks getting exasperated. "didn't see any knickers". At that point in time Dave appeared at the door with Brutus's gear wearing a pair of knickers over his head. "Whose ready for car wash" he murmured through the pants. The rest of the show went great & at the finale the guys had to get four bouncers to go into the crowd with them so that they were "safe" i.e. not molled to death. Trish was beaming from ear to ear. "Guys well done, that was a great performance", "no worries Trish" said Levi, "it's all in a shift". The dressing room door got knocked & the two girls with the leather trousers & black dress peered their heads around like a scene out of a black & white movie. "Can I help you girls" said Trish and ushered them away. "Trish when are you leaving babes" said Hero, "don't you have some hotel to go to or something to make sure the bands ok", "no Hero actually I am in no hurry at all tonight for a change" she said with a gleam in her eye.

Five minutes later she appeared back in the room, "right guys I've got to shoot, behave yourselves, no girls in the dressing room now", "Trish, what sort of boys do you think we are" said Levi looking hurt. "Levi, I know exactly what sort of boys you are" laughed Trish & disappeared. Two minutes later there was knock at the door. Brutus answered and leather & black stuck their heads in. "Come on in girls make yourselves at home" said Hero.

"Right girls" said Dave, were going to play a game, "it's called the Cinderella game", "but instead of a sparkly pair of shoes we are going to use these" Dave held up the infamous knickers.

Twenty-two

The Islands tour (part 3)

"See if I had a tenner for everytime I sat in one of these Caledonian Macbrayne ferries" Dog said to the Guys. "Yeah I know, you'd still be a poor man" replied Levi.

The Guys were on the ferry heading to sunny Arran for a one-off gig. This time though, it was actually during the summer, August to be precise & it was a lovely warm clear day. The skys were blue & the sea was blue-er. Hero was leaning over one of the railings at the side of the "ship" trying to see if he could see his reflection in the water below but he was too high up. The spray from the sea lashed about at the side of the "ship" and the odd droplet would smack you in the face. Hero wiped the spray of his face & turned to the guys, "who wants to go aft with me and do the Titanic Leonardo Di Caprio bit with me over the railings", "only If I get to be Di Caprio and you get to be the salty tart" replied Brutus. "Anyway, I'm not sure that aft is the correct direction, is it not port-side" said Brutus. "Do I look like a bloody sailor to you" asked Hero. "Well yeah actually now you come to mention it you do a bit" laughed Brutus. "Do you wannae tickle my tummy for a fiver ? Eh big boy" Brutus chuckled. "Can't be a bad life being a sailor" said Levi, "A different girl in every Port", "Yeah or boy" chortled Dog. "Listen Levi, you can't even get one girl, never mind one in every port" laughed Hero. "Levi can't get his hole in a barrel of fannies" snorted Dog. "You lot are just jealous that I've got taste, I pride myself in not going for it every time" huffed Levi. "You've no bloody choice ya ugly bastard" said Hero.

Socks came wandering back up to the Guys, "whats happening Socky boy" asked Dave. "Do you know how many people there are on this boat wearing cycling shorts" asked Socks. "No pray tell, enlighten us" replied Hero. "Well I don't know, but there is a bloody lot" said Socks. "It's all these tight spandex type ones as well", "what do you get any other type of cycling shorts then" enquired Brutus. "Oh yeah when I'm watching the Tour de France, I sit there with my bike bottle full of squash & think to myself that is a plethora of different style cycling shorts there, that guys has a lovely little woollen pair on, that dude is opting for this years in range of polyester/cotton rich blend & that boring bastard has no imagination and is sporting the usual spandex range". All the guys stared at Brutus & then each other, "I worry about you at time man, your strange" said Socks. "That's the pot calling the kettle black that" laughed Brutus. "If your not counting cycling shorts, I'm sorry I mean spandex cycling shorts, then it's bloody Shetland wool jumpers", "or Orkney wool jumpers" injected Hero. Hahahaha, the guys all laughed.

Socks did have a point though, there was an unusually large number of cyclists on-board. "I thought that Millport was meant to be their popular destination" said Hero. "Maybe there has been some sort of covert operation by the peeps who live on Arran to spread the word, covertly like, to improve the tourists numbers. They have probably being spamming websites with their propaganda. Saying that there are a cult of sex hungry cyclist chicks on Arran or something", "and you call me strange" said Brutus laughing at Hero.

The ferry pulled into Arran's Capital Broddick at 5.30pm. They were greeted by Hamish, the chap that booked the Guys. "Hamish what's the story with all the cyclists" Hero asked him. "It's some sort if annual gathering they always do it around August time" he explained, as the hordes of two wheel pedalling fanatics gathered at the far side of the port. The Guys had never seen such a gathering of Cagoules & spandex shorts in one place before. It didn't seem to faze Hamish. "Come on guys, I'll take you to your hotel". So they started to trudge after him, thinking that he was heading for his car. The guys were just foot passengers on this particular trip, which meant one very important thing. They didn't have to worry about having to drive after a nights heavy drinking. Hamish wasn't heading for a car though. He left the exit to the port, crossed the cycle infested road & walked up the path to a hotel. "Jesus that's handy" laughed Levi. "At least we won't have any excuse for missing the ferry tomorrow". "Hey don't jinx us you, touch wood when you say that" chortled Dave. The hotel was your reasonably big old fashioned traditional number. It had probably stood there at the top of a small rise, overlooking the bay for a couple of hundred years. Stick a turret or two on it & you could most definitely call it a Castle. No fancy credit card style swipe cards for the bedroom doors here. It was your massive keyring the could choke a camel. A big oval bad boy with your room number on it in gold writing, probably ahead of it's time two hundred years ago, but is the sort of key now that modern pockets aren't made for, you need a bleeding bag for this mother. I suppose it makes you think that pockets must have been made bigger back then. Saying that, thinking of all these old black & white movies with James Cagney, Humphrey Bogart & Spencer Tracy. These dudes always wore these big raincoats all the time. They had massive pockets.

A couple of grannies trudged on by with their scone shoes on & scone hats. "Don't like yours much" whispered Hero to Socks. "I'll take the one with the blue rinse" said Socks, "shit, I had my eye on her" replied Hero. Big Edwardian pictures graced the walls in the reception area. Some dude with a double barrel shotgun in one hand & what looked like a pheasant in the other hand, scowled down at them with stony eyes. "How come" said Socks to Hamish, "that the dudes in these pictures are always scowling, these always look so pissed off & serious all the time, I mean you never really see a happy chappy, going about his day, whistling or something", "eh, aye, right" answered Hamish "I can't say I've given it a lot of thought". "Well you should Man" said Socks, "I mean, think about it, these dudes are our anscestors, right", "eh yeah" said Hamish, his eyes starting to glaze over. "Well" continued Socks, "I mean, what I am driving at", "what are you driving at, you tit" laughed Hero, "no man, hear me out, what I mean to say is that, these dudes were our anscestors right", "right" said everybody in unison, including the hotel receptionist. "well, if our fathers, fathers, fathers, fathers, fathers were that serious all the time,. then the seriousness would be passed down the line from father to son right", "right" said Hero & Dog, everybody else was starting to scratch their bum, look out the window yawning etc. "well that explains a lot of shit, right, I mean bloody wars and what-not, uprisings, revolts, if every c**t was that serious all the time & not having a laugh, then that explains what a nick our country's in" Socks finished his spiel and looked satisfied with himself & look around at everybody to see if he was going to get any admiring stares or anything. "I think it's called being British" said Hamish eventually, "were a serious nation, we leave all the frivolity stuff for these European folks". "Eh ok, any chance of showing us our rooms Hamish" said Brutus glaring at Socks. "What" said Socks.

The guys were given three rooms, two in each, they paired up, Levi & Brutus, Hero & Socks & Dog & Dave. They freshened up, got a change of clothes & headed down to the bar for a pre-dinner swally. They had a pint each & then got stuck into to some nice grilled salmon with wild rice, washed down with a bottle of nice white wine from Chile & then cheesecake for desert. They moved over to the conservatory at the front of the hotel to have coffee & after dinner mints. The view was spectacular. The sun was going down and the sea was very calm, no wind at all. A few seagulls were pattering around on the hotel sign at the front of the grounds. A few cyclists sped by, no cagoules, it was too nice. "Looks like they missed the ferry" said Hero. "Guys this is a bad idea, a heavy meal, a couple of swallies & now coffee in here, i'm so relaxed I can't be bothered doing the gig" said Brutus. "that's fine, we'll just leave you, your shite anyway" chortled Levi. Hamish appeared, "Hi guys, you fancy another pint, we've got time", they looked at each other, "aye ok then, on ye go" said Dave, Brutus sighed. "Whose the unlucky guys that got room fifteen then" asked Hamish. Dave & Dog looked at each other, "Dog and me, why" asked Dave. "Well, there is a bit of a story about room fifteen" said Hamish with a glint in his eye. "Pray tell, what is that then" said Dog, with more than a small feeling of woe. "Haud the bus a second" said Dave, "before you start, this isn't going to be a moment out of the movie the Shining is it, is there going to be some doing bit of gear waiting for us in the shower when we get back from the gig & then when we get a bit over amorous she turns into something out of the Night of the Living Dead", "shut up and let the guy talk Dave", said Levi.

"Well" said Hamish, "rumour has it that there was a guest staying in that room many, many moons ago, a Man. He was seemingly a travelling salesman, living out of one suitcase & in the other suitcase, he carried his wares. He was going from door to door selling, well whatever he was selling. At night he would drink in the local bars, eat at the hotel & sleep at the hotel. Nobody knows what sort of person he was, the stories don't attribute his character traits, just his routine. Housecleaning were doing their normal daily routine, replacing the sheets & tidying the rooms. When she knocked his door, there was no answer, so she used her skeleton pass key.

He was lying naked on the bed, dead, with both wrists slashed & the open razor lying on the floor next to the bed. He was lying with his feet together & his arms at right angles over the bed, depicting the crucifixion scene.

"So" said Hero, "So some guy many moons ago was having a shit time of it trying to sell glamorous women's undies to a thermal undies, damart wearing society.

He realised that he was onto plums, his wife had left him because he was a shit provider, he couldn't see his kids anymore & his football team were bottom of the league again", "aye add arms and legs to it will you" said Dog, "more like slashed arms & legs" said Socks. "He wouldn't be the first Guy to commit hari kari" said Hero. "Let me finsh" said Hamish, "what there's more" laughed Dave, "oh great". "Just about anybody that has stayed in that room since, has told reception in the morning that they could swear that they heard a mans voice in the room, some have been that spooked that they have demanded they be moved to a different room in the middle of the night". "Of course the hotel doesn't make a issue of telling the guests the story, they don't want to frighten folk away & lose business", "aye cheers Hamish, were so glad you felt the need to tell us", laughed Hero. Hamish just smirked. "Hamish, is this where you tell us the punch line" said Dave. "What punch line" said Hamish. "The one where you tells us what the ghost of the man was saying, was it get your French knickers & underwired bra here, three for a pound-a", everybody laughed. "What a bag of baws" said Dog unbelievingly & looked nervously at Dave. "Yeah bag of baws" repeated Dave, looking at the floor.

They made their way to the gig, Hamish took Hero, Socks & Dave in his car & the others went in a taxi. The gig was about forty minutes away on the other side of the Island. They followed the rather needing of repair windy road, they passed through quaint villages with smoke whisping out of the chimneys. It might have been summer, but on the Islands the breeze still comes in from the sea at nights & casts a chill over the island. They passed streams, which were snaking down from the hills into the salty sea water. They passed big open fields with your usual scattering of cows & sheep & the odd horse with a coat thrown over them. They arrived at the gig eventually; it was a largish community centre. Another strange venue once again for the Highlanders to get their boabeys oot in. It was rammed, a bustle of noise & faces turning towards them as they made their way through the crowd. There was a small but high stage at the end, at the back of which there was a kind of store room where the guys were getting changed. It smelled of something stale, there was a bingo thingy which you put the balls in and turn them around in the corner. There was an old piano. Dog opened the lid & tried a few of the keys, it sounded pretty good still. They probably had piano recital's once a month on a Wednesday night. Brutus walked over & pushed Dog out the way &

started doing the chopsticks. Hero pushed Brutus out the way & started bashing out non-sensical notes & making a face and singing "I was sitting at the piano the other day" doing his Jimmy Durante impersonation.

"Good evening ladies, how are you feeling this evening", Dave started his spiel. "They sound lively enough" said Socks, "bread & butter" said Levi. "Forget about the stage for the opening routine" said Dog, "there's no way we can do a five man opener". "Just you guys do it" said Hero, "I'll get ready and go on straight after you file off". The show went smooth as a nut. The Arran crowd were mental & loved every minute of it. The guys were doing autographs at the end of the show. You always got that when you went on tour, sometimes even back in Glasgow you got asked. "Furry boots are ye fae like" asked a Shetland wool wearing bonny lassie. "Glasgow" answered Socks. "Glasgae, yer aw ra wae fae Glasgae" said the girl. "Jeannie they braw boys are aw ra wae fae Glasgae", "Glasgae, are ye really boys, whit a distance, where are you staying" asked Jeannie, "back at yours for a party darling" said Dog, "hahaha ma man wouldnae be very pleased aboot that" replied Jeannie. "where are ye staying" repeated Jeannies pal, "were staying in the hotel with the ghost" replied Socks. "Oww are ye staying at the Burnbrae then" she replied. "Well is that the hotel with the ghost" said Socks looking at the other guys, "aye the Burnbrae overlooking the port" said Jeannie. "Do you want to take us back for a drink" asked Jeannies pal, "eh well that would be lovely" said Socks, "but Hamish is taking three of us with the gear & the other three are getting a taxi with the rest of the gear" continued Socks. "Ach it's too far, all that way to the other side of ra Island" said Jeannie to her pal.

Hamish appeared to take the guys back. "Say goodbye girls", Jeannies pal went up to Hero to give him a kiss goodbye & Hero moved in to give her a peck in the lips & she just got wired in, one minute later she came up for air, she giggled & Her and Jeannie waved goodbye and disappeared back into the main room. "That was the bouncers bird" said Hamish. "Shit shit" said Hero looking nervous. On the way back they couldn't see f**k all. "Don't they have street lights on the Island Hamish" asked Socks. "Yeah there's loads round in Broddick" he laughed. "Just as well for the cats eyes eh" said Hero. They got back to the hotel & dumped their gear in the rooms & then headed for the bar. There was a couple of guests still sitting drinking. Just as well or they would had to wake the bar guy up. They sat to about 3am going through a few cask ales before moving onto the spirits. Socks was first to throw the towel in - lightweight. The rest all followed within half an hour.

Hero awoke at 5am with the bedroom door getting banged. He opened it to a frightened looking Dave. "What's up with you" said Hero, "it's true, it's bloody true", "what's true" said Socks waking up. "The bloody ghost of that guy" said Dave, "I can hear him talking, he just keeps going on & on, it's feckin creaping me out". "Haha your at it ya fanny, thanks a lot for waking us up" said Hero. "I'm not feckin joking, I'm totally freaked out". "Where's Dog" asked Socks. "He's out for the count, he's pished" said Dave still shaking. "I'm going back to sleep, goodnight ya nut" said Socks to Dave. Dave climbed in beside Socks, "what the f**k do you think your doing" Socks shouted, "please Socks, i've nowhere to sleep" replied Dave, "just make sure you keep these boxers on boy" said Socks.

The guys were just nodding back off to sleep when there door got banged again. "What now" shouted Hero jumping up and answering the door. Dog rushed in and slammed the door behind him. "What the f**k" exclaimed Socks. "It's true, it's true" shouted Dog, "Dave, Dave I thought the ghost had got you", "eh" said Socks. "The ghost it was talking to me" said Dog. "Why didn't you go to some other c**ts room you, it's not a bloody party in here you know" exclaimed Hero getting annoyed. "What was the ghost saying then" asked Socks with more than a hint of sarcasm. "It just kept repeating a womans name over and over again" said Dog, "what bloody name" said Hero.

"Jeannie" said Dog.

Twenty-three

(The Veterans)

Socks climbed out of bed, had a long stretch, went for a piss, washed & dried his hands & then looked at himself in the mirror. Jesus, talk about facial changes. He must have gone through about ten in the last fifteen years of his stripping career. It was the end of 2006. Did he still have it, still have that special something ? Nah, don't think so son. Bald apart from the side & that widow's type peak thing at the front & a nice not over the top set of side burns. Eyes were still bright though. How were the crow's feet, not great, just accentuated laughter lines really. Hows the bod, top off, yeah the old teats have tightened up a good bit, still pretty tight. Hows the legs, yip the quads and hams have always been pretty ok, shite calves though. Can't complain too much, have really trained hard the last half of this year. The teats were quite saggy but have definitely tightened up.

Saying that though, these other two fuds weren't any better. Hero was getting a bit beefy around the midrift, although he has been trying to diet. Still a big lad though in a kind off wrestler physique way. As for Levi, well Levi was always a bit of a bag of nails. Didn't train worth a f**k but still managed to maintain a half decent frame. I suppose his dance moves make up for it, but not for a long time.

You will have observed that I said the other two fuds & not the other four fuds ! Yes unfortunately Brutus & Dog fell by the wayside, as did our legendary DJ/MC Dave. You see the whole stripping market changed drastically over the years. The demand for the five man shows faded or should I say the amount of money that the venues were willing to pay out faded. This resulted in a rota system where gigs were concerned. We started going out as first a four man team & then a three man team, which is the current set up for today. The two man gigs & one man gigs also got a bit quieter. Dave was first to go, He had been working full time selling cars & was doing pretty mad hours at times. The gigs became a hassle to him. He became a taxi driver & got married to a wee darlin.So he was replaced by Marty, no relation to the crew dude at the start of the book or Marti Pellow. Then Brutus went, he had met a lovely girl & fell head over heals. She wasn't too mad about the stripping, so that was that. He moved into his Dad's old shoes & started driving trucks. Got married, went to London for a while before coming back to the land of the brave & the free. He now has two beautiful boys. Dog was last too go, He had kept his hand in boxing, so he went back to the ring for a while doing a few amateur bouts but mainly getting paid to spar. He ended up being a trainer for a reasonably talented Glasgow boy. He remarried to another diamond gal & has just recently had a wee boy.

That leaves us three fuds. Levi although still stripping went back to working down the sewers, got engaged, is due to get married next year is hopefully moving to Australia to get a better way of life. Seemingly there is a big demand for sewage workers down under (boom boom). He also has two lovely boys. Hero, also still stripping went back to work on the doors. He never got married & has no kids (yet), although he has a lovely long term devoted girlfriend, so who knows. Socks although still definitely kicking the arse out of the stripping went back to working full time in the golf ball factory, putting dimples on the balls. He married the delicious Hester, although things didn't work out & they went their separate ways. He still stays in touch & they are good friends. He is still close to her son Connor. Rumour has it that he fancies himself as a bit of a writer.

Nowadays the fans & the media/press, the autographs are a thing of the past. We are no longer in the limelight. Which is exactly what we want. You see as you get older you change, things that seem important when you are young no longer hold that fascination. Nowadays we are quite happy to go about our daily business quietly or as quiet as three veteran strippers can. It has been a rollercoaster ride. I wouldn't change it for anything or anybody. Once a year, whatever happens during the year or however busy we are. We always meet up at Xmas the six of us & talk for the UK.

It's not over to the fat lady sings. "Does anybody know what that is meant to mean" said Socks, "It's not over to the fat lady sings", "who cares" said Hero. "No think about it" said Socks, "It's not over", "what's not over", "to the fat lady sings". "Socks, does it really f**king matter, who cares" said Dave. "I think that what it means is that when the fat lady sings everybody stops to listen" said Socks. "Why do they stop to listen" asked Dog, "because man, because usually big fat people who are singers are really good aren't they, something to do with the lung size or something, especially on birds" replied Socks. "So" said Brutus, "so, so if they are that good at chanting, then because everybody stops to listen. Then whatever they were doing before that, drinking,eating, talking, going to the loo, that's the it's not over part". "Aaah" said Levi.

"Shut up ya fanny" said Dave.

The End

www.ingramcontent.com/pod-product-compliance
Lightning Source LLC
LaVergne TN
LVHW091001080826
845145LV00003B/1082